Evangelship captures the heart of the Great Commission in a fresh and practical way. Larry Perez shows how evangelism and discipleship aren't competing tasks but a Spirit-led lifestyle lived out in everyday relationships. This book will empower believers to move beyond programs and step confidently into the mission field of their homes, workplaces, and communities. It's timely, authentic, and deeply aligned with the heart of the church.

WILFREDO (CHOCO) DE JESÚS, executive director,
Assemblies of God U.S. Missions

In *Evangelship*, Larry Perez gives us the gift of seeing Jesus at work in the lives around us. As I read each page, I felt myself pulled back into the neighborhood where God is at work, drawing people to himself. Read this book and grow deeper in the ways of Jesus, renew your passion for mission, and learn the ways of listening and of being present in a place. I truly loved this book.

DAVID FITCH, Lindner Chair of Theology and
Mission, Northern Seminary; author, *Faithful Presence*

Evangelship is a glorious invitation to an integrated journey. With grace and conviction, Larry Perez reminds us that we don't have to choose between evangelism and discipleship. The Christian call is a both/and call to join God in his mission to change the world. This book is a gift for all those who have longed for a vibrant model of a deeper life of holistic gospel engagement that heals our city and our world. It's a must-read!

GABRIEL AND JEANETTE SALGUERO,
cofounders, National Latino Evangelical Coalition

Evangelship meets a critical need in Jesus' church today. Some churches either do well at bringing people to faith in Christ *or* making disciples. Although the majority of Christian churches do not do either very well, it is rare to find those effective at *both* evangelism and discipleship. *Evangelship* is a practical and inspirational tool for any ministry leader who wants to fulfill all of Jesus' mission for his church. The book is filled with practical, biblical, and well-researched instructions, plus inspiring examples of what it looks like to help the people all around us become fully committed and mature Christ-followers.

ALAN EHLER, pastor and professor;
author, *How to Make Big Decisions Wisely*

Evangelship offers a refreshing and timely reminder that evangelism and discipleship are not separate tasks but part of one continuous journey toward Jesus. Rather than presenting faith as a formula or method, Perez calls us to a way of being—with authenticity, presence, and love. He invites readers to see evangelism not as getting people to "make a decision" or attend church, but as walking alongside others toward a Person—Christ himself. As a Latino engaged in urban mission, I find this book deeply valuable—especially for Christians living on mission in complex, diverse city contexts. Perez's vision honors the slow, relational, and incarnational work of God among our neighbors. He reminds us that people stand at different points along the spiritual path, each with their own awareness and openness to God. Our role is to discern how God is already present and to walk with others toward Christ. *Evangelship* beautifully blurs the line between evangelism and discipleship, inviting everyday believers to embody the gospel through genuine care, intentional relationships, and conversations that dignify and humanize others.

ROBERT GUERRERO, vice president
movement catalyst, Redeemer City to City

Larry Perez didn't just write the "best in class" paper on evangelism; he lives it. From turning a routine barber shop visit into an opportunity to make disciples to opening mission fields in local factories, Larry demonstrates how to actualize the evangelship movement. Dr. Perez has vast experience in discipling the unchurched. Engage this groundbreaking book in your personal and leadership development.

REV. DR. ROBERT J. PRICE, JR., professor emeritus,
Evangelism and Urban Ministry, Northern Seminary

Larry Perez has given the church a tremendous gift. I love what he's doing here, bringing evangelism and discipleship back together as a way of life, not a set of programs. He's not only offering us a pattern for the Spirit's formation, but he's also living it in the everyday places he calls *wells*. This book is honest, practical, and deeply Spirit–tuned, inviting us to follow Jesus into the ordinary spaces where lives are changed.

JEREMY SIMS, professor, Spiritual Formation; program director, MAMEX and DMin Cohorts, Southeastern University

When you read this book, you're not simply turning pages — you're stepping into a journey that begins with your heart, reshapes your eyes so you can truly see people, empowers your feet to go where God sends you, guides your hands to meet real needs, and releases your voice to speak the gospel with compassion and courage.

This is more than a book. It's a blueprint for reclaiming the very thing God designed the church to do—reach people, disciple them, and change the world, one life at a time. And Larry Perez lives every word he teaches. His passion for evangelism and discipleship is not a theory; it is a life lived with purpose, consistency, humility, and courage.

My prayer is that this book ignites you the way it ignites me—from your heart … to your eyes … to your feet … to your hands … to your voice—so you can step fully into the life God intended.

LLOYD ZEIGLER, lead pastor, Victorious Life Church, Waco, Texas

I loved reading this book. Larry Perez's love and passion for Jesus and for people jumped off every page, helping readers to better understand the powerful connection between sharing the good news and living it out so that others are moved to live like Jesus themselves.

NOEL CASTELLANOS, president, Camino Alliance

Evangelship is a compelling and timely paradigm shift for the twenty-first-century church. By exposing the false divide between evangelism and discipleship, Dr. Larry Perez invites us into the mission-shaped life envisioned in the New Testament. With the insight of a scholar, the heart of a pastor, and the experience of a frontline practitioner, he not only critiques our inherited categories, he also equips us with tools and practices that cultivate a people deeply formed in the life and mission of Jesus.

JAY PIKE, lead pastor, The Bridge Church, Texas

Evangelship is a timely and much-needed wake-up call to the modern church. Using the power of stories, Larry Perez masterfully weaves together evangelism, discipleship, and mentorship into a continual, rotating cycle—each one reinforcing and empowering the others. This intertwined model is not only biblical but also essential, and he presents it with clarity, conviction, and deep spiritual insight.

In a time when many churches have either abandoned or unintentionally ignored this foundational pattern, *Evangelship* reestablishes what Scripture has always revealed: that the health, growth, and effectiveness of every believer—and every church—depends on this dynamic cycle. When evangelism leads to discipleship, and discipleship leads to more evangelism, the church becomes vibrant, multiplying, and aligned with Christ's mission.

This book is more than a teaching—it is a blueprint for transformation. *Evangelship* is the absolute key to raising strong, mature believers and building thriving, mission-focused churches. Every pastor, ministry leader, and follower of Jesus should read it, embrace it, and put it into practice.

I highly and wholeheartedly recommend *Evangelship*. It carries a powerful truth the church urgently needs to recover.

REV. PHILLIP B. SCHNEIDER, former Illinois
district superintendent, Assemblies of God

Larry Perez has given the church a gift in *Evangelship*, calling us back to the heart of Jesus where evangelism and discipleship are not separated but lived as a beautiful rhythm in everyday life. I am grateful for my friend Larry and this timely book that teaches us how to love God and neighbors.

DAVID DOCUSEN, author, Neighborliness;
president, International Ministry Network

Pastor Larry Perez's passion for souls is contagious. *Evangelship* will remind you that it's not just about encountering Christ but also about committing to follow him to become like him. I recommend every pastor give this book as a gift to their outreach teams and ministries as a source of inspiration and a license to be creative and passionate about sharing the gospel.

RICO ALTIERY, executive pastor,
New Life Covenant Church, Chicago

This book hits with a rhythm the church has been missing. It reminds us that ministry isn't just what happens on a stage; it's what breaks out in the lives of people, in the barbershops, the coffee shops, the everyday corners where the pulse never stops. The stories carry weight, the insights have flow, and the message pushes leaders to move with intention instead of waiting for crowds to come to them. It's raw, it's real, and it's a needed beat for anyone serious about taking the gospel to the world and out into the streets.

DR. EDWIN MELENDEZ, lead pastor,
Culture City Church, Cicero, Illinois

Larry Perez brings evangelism and discipleship back together where they belong—in the real, everyday spaces of life. *Evangelship* calls us to step out, listen deeply, build authentic relationships, and meet people where they are, just like Jesus did. This book is full of practical wisdom and real stories that inspired me, and I believe it will challenge and equip anyone who wants to see the church come alive beyond its walls.

Perez doesn't just write about evangelism and discipleship—he lives it out and raises up others to do the same, both in churches and right where they work. *Evangelship* is a fresh, practical call to bring the gospel into real life—by listening, serving, and meeting people where they are. Larry's stories and example will encourage and equip you to live on mission wherever God sends you.

BRIAN DYE, executive director, Legacy Disciple

evangelship

evangelship

RECLAIMING GOD'S DESIGN FOR EVANGELISM & DISCIPLESHIP

LAWRENCE PEREZ

First published in 2026 by 100Movements Publishing
100Movements.com
Copyright © 2026 by Lawrence Perez

Library of Congress Control Number: 2026904392

ISBN: 978-1-955142-79-3 (paperback)
ISBN: 978-1-955142-81-6 (hardback)
ISBN: 978-1-955142-80-9 (eBook)

Cover design and interior design by Jude May
Cover image © t_kimura | iStock

100Movements Publishing
An imprint of 100Movements
Cody, Wyoming
100Movements.com

access free content online

- **Five Small Group Video Sessions:** A dedicated video for key evangelship principles.
- **Small Group Discussion Guide:** A downloadable guide with questions for each session.

Find everything at:
www.evangelship.com

contents

foreword

In *Evangelship*, Lawrence Perez has given us a timely and practical contribution to our understanding of evangelism and discipleship. The church continues to wrestle with how to reach people meaningfully while also forming them into mature followers of Jesus. Perez brings these concerns together with clarity. His central insight—that evangelism and discipleship grow best as one unified way of life—sets the tone for a book that is both accessible and deeply aligned with the heart of Christian mission.

The ideas in this book resonated deeply with me, affirming themes that have guided my own work, particularly in *Reframation* and *Disciplism*. Like those works, this book champions the call to recover a thoroughly missional approach to evangelism by reframing evangelism as an aspect of discipleship. Perez carries this impulse forward with fresh clarity and insight, extending the vision in meaningful ways. Crucially, he grounds it in the daily actions and relationships that shape real ministry, showing how relationships, shared routines, curiosity, and consistent presence create the conditions where people discover Jesus and learn to follow him. This is a way of seeing mission that grows from real life rather than from programs or events, a practicality that is one of *Evangelship's* greatest strengths.

This book does not rely on theory but draws from real-life stories to show how friendship, listening, and patient accompaniment open doors for spiritual growth. These stories demonstrate how the mission of Jesus grows through ordinary conversations, small gestures of care, and the willingness to remain available over time. Perez emphasizes that spiritual maturity emerges through shared journey—around tables, in neighborhoods, within everyday rhythms. This is where faith is formed and where trust grows. When evangelism flows from these same spaces, it gains depth, credibility, and genuine impact. Real change grows from committed disciples who help others become disciples. Anyone seeking a picture of evangelism that feels natural and sustainable will find encouragement here.

Evangelship offers a vision of mission that can be readily embraced by pastors, church planters, ministry teams, and everyday Christians. It brings the Great Commission within reach by reminding us that we already live among the people God has entrusted to our care. With thoughtful guidance and practical steps, Perez helps readers cultivate habits that open pathways to meaningful spiritual conversations and long-term transformation.

I believe this book will serve the church powerfully in our time. It calls us back to a way of life that reflects Jesus' own pattern of walking with people, investing deeply, and trusting the slow work of God. My hope is that many will pick up *Evangelship*, take its guidance seriously, and discover renewed confidence for the mission we all share—to proclaim and demonstrate the gospel of the reign of God in our Lord Jesus Christ.

Alan Hirsch

Author of numerous books on missional spirituality, leadership, and organization; cofounder, Movement Leaders Collective, Forge Missional Training Network, and 5Q Collective

introduction
find the wells

Where are the wells? Where are those places that God is waiting for us to join him and encounter others on his mission toward living out the Great Commission? When I first felt the call to pastor in January of 2007, I had this big dream to plant a church in the western suburbs of Chicago. But there was one question I couldn't shake: *Where are the wells?*

In John 4, Jesus meets a Samaritan woman at a well. You know the story—it wasn't just about water. The well was where people gathered, where life happened. And for her, it became the place where she met God in a way that changed everything. That got me thinking: *Where are the wells today?* Where are the spaces in my community where the unchurched naturally gather? Where is God already showing up, waiting for us to engage?

Growing up in Logan Square, Chicago, my wife, Yezenia, and I knew exactly where the "wells" were. In our *barrio*, it was the parks, the mall, the corner stores, and the local gyms.[1] These were the places where people hung out, shared stories, and built relationships. But when we moved to the western suburbs, everything felt different. The vibe, the rhythm of life, even the "wells" were unfamiliar. We couldn't just bring our old mindset into this new community. We had to ask ourselves all over again: *Where are the wells?*

And here's what stands out to me about Jesus at the well. He didn't stumble on that spot by accident. He chose it. Scripture says, "He had to go through Samaria" (John 4:4), meaning it wasn't a detour; it was a key step in God's plan for reaching all people. Jesus put himself right in the middle of someone else's daily life. And he didn't come with flashy programs or quick fixes. He came with a conversation, a moment of connection that would transform her life—and through her, an entire community.

That's the blueprint, isn't it? Jesus didn't wait for people to come to him; he went to where they were, to their wells. For us who are hearing the missional call, it's the same. Whether it's the local coffee shop, a basketball court, or a mom's group at the library, we've got to find the places where life is happening and step into those spaces with intentionality.

The Barbershop That Became My Church

One of the first wells I found? A barbershop.

Now, let me just say—if you know me, you know I don't have much hair. But trust me, I let whatever I had grow just long enough so I'd have an excuse to get a cut at a famous barbershop in the greater Chicago area. This wasn't just any barbershop. It was the place to be. People traveled from all over just to get their fade done by the best in town. The vibe was electric—rap music blasting, TVs everywhere, kids running around, and guys stepping outside through the back door for … well, let's just say, a little "fresh air." Every now and then, someone would come in selling everything from socks to PlayStations and watches. It was a whole *scene*.

And I loved it.

At the time, I was a bivocational pastor—working as a probation officer for Cook County by day and planting a church by night (and basically every other free moment). The first time I walked into the barbershop, I wasn't there to preach or pass out flyers. I was there to get to know the people, to listen, to build real relationships.

Donny, the owner, was the first person I connected with. He gave me a fresh cut (or at least, as fresh as my limited hair allowed), and we just *talked*. I didn't start with ministry. I didn't push church. I just asked about *him*—his story, his business, his life.

When I told Donny I was a probation officer, his whole demeanor shifted. A lot of the guys who worked there had been through the system or were dealing with cases at my courthouse. To them, I wasn't just some random guy—I was someone who understood their world. That opened a door.

Week after week, I kept showing up, and, little by little, relationships formed. Soon, Donny and I were talking about life, family, even faith. Eventually, he started introducing me to his friends and workers. They knew I was a probation officer *and* a pastor. And from time to time, I'd ask Donny, "Hey, man, anything I can pray for?"

That simple question changed everything.

Over time, I was able to guide him on personal matters, pray over his new building, and be there for guys who were dealing with relationship struggles, legal issues, or just life in general. Some needed attorneys. Some needed prayer. Some just needed someone to listen. Ministry wasn't happening inside a church building—it was happening right there in the middle of the barbershop.

Then one day, after months of meeting, I asked Donny if he'd be open to discipleship. He said yes. We'd meet up, at times do communion, and dig into the teachings of Jesus. One Thursday, I showed up early for our usual meeting. Donny was running late, so I figured maybe it wasn't happening that day. But when he finally walked in, he turned to his waiting clients and said, "Yo, I gotta meet with my pastor first—give me thirty minutes."

That was the moment I knew: God was ready to move into his heart.

We sat down, talked, and right there, in the middle of the barbershop, Donny got on his knees and surrendered his life to Jesus. The whole shop became a place of discipleship. Donny set up a little shelf in the front and called it *Larry's pulpit*. Any time I rolled through, the barbers would turn their chairs to face me while I shared a quick word. I kept it short, less than ten minutes, but it was enough. Enough for people to hear. Enough for people to start asking for prayer. Enough for lives to start changing.

The gospel was moving in the shop, and so were my relationships with the barbers. Conversations turned into connections, and connections turned into discipleship. Before I knew it, another barbershop opened its doors, giving me a fresh space to build, invest, and evangelize. As trust grew, I wasn't just cutting it up with them about life—I was praying with them, introducing them to attorneys when they needed help, and being there in real, tangible ways.

But it wasn't just about the shop. I was out in the streets—literally—praying and walking the community, getting to know the heartbeat of the city before launching the church. I built relationships with local business owners, factory workers, gas station attendants—you name it. God even opened doors to connect with the mayor, the chief of police, and the superintendents of the high schools near where we planned to plant.

Discovering Evangelship

I didn't have a name for what I was doing back then—I was just following Jesus and meeting people where they were. But later, I realized I was practicing something powerful. I call it *evangelship*—the integration of *evangelism* and *discipleship*.

For too long, the church has treated evangelism and discipleship like apples and oranges—good on their own but belonging to entirely separate categories, leading to fragmented efforts. We hold outreach events to "win souls," but then what? Or we focus on discipleship, but only for the people already inside our churches. But what if this separation was never God's design? The truth is, the two are inseparable, woven into the single, life-giving process modeled by Jesus. They are not two different fruits to be compared but one whole fruit, always connected from the start. They are meant to grow from the same tree and carry the complete flavor of the Great Commission.

This fragmentation is especially costly because our culture has shifted. Society is more distracted than ever—caught up in social media, entertainment, and a growing disinterest in faith. Because of this noise, the old ways of evangelism aren't working. People are less interested in crossing a formal threshold to hear a religious invitation, and our programs can't compete with the tailored experiences of modern consumerism. Therefore, evangelism and discipleship can't be separate steps; they have to be integrated into one authentic, life-on-life connection—just like Jesus modeled at the well.

Evangelship is the answer. It's not an event. It's a lifestyle that integrates evangelism and discipleship in a way that isn't about making converts but making disciples. The unification of these two entities is the foundation of this book. It isn't just theory. It's my journey—what I've lived, what I've seen, and what I believe can reignite a passion for reaching people.

Through stories, insights, and research, I'll share how to implement strategies that lead to an integrated model of evangelism and discipleship reflective of the biblical model Jesus practiced.[2] My prayer is that you'll see that you are the event—wherever you are.

So let me ask you: *Where are the wells in your city?* Where are the unchurched gathering? Where is God already at work, inviting you to show up and build relationships? Because here's the thing: When you meet people at their well, you're not just offering them water—you're offering them *living water*. And that changes everything.

So, let's go find the wells. Because that's where Jesus is already waiting.

BECOME THE MESSAGE

1

inhale, exhale

FOR YEARS, FOOTBALL was my life. I started in grammar school and kept going all the way to my freshman year of college. Defense was my thing. I loved the rush of the game, the adrenaline of landing a big hit. But one particular moment on the field taught me a lesson I didn't expect—a lesson about breathing.

It was fourth down and our opponent (who was on offense) decided to punt the ball to us. At that moment I was locked in, ready to block the ball. The ball snapped, and I saw a wide-open hole, clear as day. I knew I had it. I was going to make the play. But just as I leaped to block the ball, *bam!* Out of nowhere, the opposing player hit me so hard, I flipped in the air and landed flat on my back.

That's when it happened: I got the wind knocked out of me. If you've ever been there, you know the feeling. I couldn't breathe. It was like I inhaled but forgot how to exhale. No matter how hard I tried, I couldn't force the air out. And let

Inhale without exhale can kill you.

me tell you, I learned something in that moment—inhale without exhale can kill you.

Is it possible that the Western church needs to learn a similar lesson? Could it be that, when it comes to evangelism and discipleship, we've forgotten how to breathe?

Here's the thing: Breathing is a rhythm. Inhale, exhale. You can't do one without the other. And this rhythm is a powerful metaphor for the church when it comes to understanding evangelship. *Discipleship is the inhale*—taking in the Word, growing in faith, for spiritual formation. *Evangelism is the exhale*—reaching out, sharing the gospel, pouring ourselves out into the lives of others.

Evangelship is the integration of evangelism and discipleship in a relational lifestyle that guides others toward becoming disciples of Jesus who, in turn, make disciples.

Evangelship is the integration of evangelism and discipleship in a relational lifestyle that guides others toward becoming disciples of Jesus who, in turn, make disciples. It is not a singular event but an ongoing process, deeply embedded in community life.

The problem is that some churches are all about the exhale. They're constantly pouring out but never stopping to take in. Others are stuck on the inhale, focusing on spiritual growth but never stepping out to share what they've received. Either way, it's unsustainable. Just like I couldn't survive on that football field without both inhaling and exhaling, the church can't thrive unless evangelism and discipleship are integrated, working together in a healthy rhythm. The beauty of breathing is in the balance. And when we find that rhythm, we're not just surviving—we're living, moving, and making an eternal impact.

The Gospel of Luke shows us this rhythm in action when it puts the story of the Good Samaritan (Luke 10:25–37) right next to the story of Mary and Martha (Luke 10:38–42). The Good Samaritan is the pure exhale—pouring out time, resources, and love in active service to a stranger in need. Then, immediately after, Mary demonstrates the inhale—sitting at the feet of Jesus, prioritizing her relationship with him. We can't survive without both.

So, here's the question: What's your rhythm? Are you inhaling but forgetting to exhale? Or are you exhaling so much that you're running on empty?

Inhale. Exhale. Let's not forget how to breathe.

The Bigger Story

When we think about faith, we often start with Jesus—and that's not wrong. But the bigger story actually starts much earlier. Back in the first pages of the Bible, in Genesis 12, God makes a bold move. He calls a man named Abram and invites him into something massive—something that would impact every generation to come.

Let's take a look:

> Go from your country, your people and your father's household to the land I will show you.
> I will make you into a great nation, and I will bless you;
> I will make your name great, and you will be a blessing.
> I will bless those who bless you, and whoever curses you I will curse;
> and all peoples on earth will be blessed through you.

GENESIS 12:1–3

This is more than just a personal promise. It's the start of God's mission to bless the entire world—and Abraham (God changes his name later) is invited to be part of it. Abraham not only becomes God's first disciple, but he also has his own conversion and eventually is invited to join God on a mission. Notice how the blessing doesn't stop with him. God blesses Abraham *so that* he can become a blessing to others.

> **God blesses people not to stockpile that blessing but to pass it on.**

This pattern shows up again and again in Scripture. God blesses people not to stockpile that blessing but to pass it on. You could say God's plan has always been: "I bless you, so others can be blessed through you." God doesn't bless *to* but instead blesses *through!*

From the beginning, God's heart was for *everyone*. Even though he chose one man, and eventually one nation, the goal wasn't exclusivity—it was multiplication. Abraham's story is the launchpad for a global mission. As one scholar put it, God didn't call Israel to be a *reservoir* of blessing but a *river*.[1] The blessing was never meant to be stored up. It was meant to flow outward.

What's wild is that Abraham wasn't exactly a religious superstar. He came from a family of idol worshippers (Joshua 24:2), and there's no record of him doing anything impressive before God called him. He wasn't chosen because of his credentials—he was chosen because of God's grace. That's what makes this story so hopeful. If God can use a man like Abraham to bless the world, he can use *anyone*, including you.

The Blueprint of Jesus

And here's the thing: This mission didn't end with Abraham. It didn't even end with Israel. It found its fulfillment in Jesus.

Fast forward to the New Testament, and the very first sentence in the Gospel of Matthew says this: "Jesus the Messiah, the son of David, the son of Abraham" (Matthew 1:1). That's not just a genealogy. That's a flashing sign pointing us back to the promise in Genesis 12. Jesus is the ultimate "seed of Abraham." Through him, the blessing extends to *everyone*—not just one nation, not just one culture, not just the religious elite.

And now, anyone who follows Jesus is part of that mission, too. The apostle Paul puts it this way: "If you belong to Christ, then you are Abraham's seed, and heirs according to the promise" (Galatians 3:29).

We are invited into the very same blessing-passing movement that started with Abraham. We don't just receive grace, healing, and hope for ourselves—we're sent out to bring that to others.

Jesus didn't give his followers a marketing plan or a five-step conversion program. He said, "Go and make disciples of all nations" (Matthew 28:19). That word *disciple* simply means learner or follower. And Jesus' method was simple: Walk with people. Teach them. Show them how to live. And then send them out to do the same.

That's the blueprint:

1. Follow Jesus.
2. Be transformed by him.
3. Join him in his mission.

This is evangelship. Not a flashy campaign but a lifestyle. Not pushing people to "make a decision" but walking with them as they discover who Jesus is and learn to live like him.

Living It Out

Here's where it gets exciting: When you walk with someone in faith, not only will their life change, but they'll also eventually do the same for someone else. That's how the blessing multiplies.

God's mission hasn't changed since Genesis 12. He's still in the business of blessing people—and he still invites ordinary people to be part of it.

When we live with that kind of intention, when we make space for others to discover who God is, we're stepping into the same story Abraham did. And just like him, we don't have to have it all figured out. We just have to say yes to the journey.

Everything has a starting point, a genesis. For me, walking into barbershops to talk to strangers wasn't something that came naturally. I wasn't born with a boldness to approach people. It was something I learned over time—and honestly, it came with understanding why it was important to be ready to live out the gospel.

One of my biggest teachers in this was my late pastor, William Vazquez. To me, he was the *greatest* example of evangelship, and I'm so thankful for all the time I spent with him. He didn't talk about reaching others; he *lived* it. It was natural to him. I remember watching him talk to anyone and everyone, not as a preacher but as a friend. When he'd take his wife to the salon, he would help out around the store, shoveling snow at the entrance in the winter and sweeping the salon floor in every season. Through the relationships William built at the salon and the way he served, the owner of the shop eventually started coming to the church and also led others to know Christ and discipled others as well.

He lived by this simple truth: "By serving the people, we serve the Lord." It wasn't a theory for him; it was a lifestyle. Discipleship evangelism wasn't something he told me to do. He didn't give me a list of "how-tos" on evangelism. He *acted* it out. His life was a constant reminder of *why* evangelship matters, and that's something that stuck with me.

Start with Why

Here's what I've come to believe: The *why* behind what we do is the key to everything. You can teach someone the *how*, but it's the *why* that gives power to the action. As is widely known from Simon Sinek's "Start with Why" concept, true inspiration and momentum come when we start from the core belief (the *why*) rather than the method (the *how*).[2]

So, before we dive into the *how* of evangelship, let's take a step back and anchor ourselves in the core *why*: It isn't a program or a duty—it's the radical, transforming love of Jesus. Following him changes everything. When we start there, we move people from simply being informed to being fundamentally transformed. We're not simply trying to save souls; we're trying to make disciples who embody and multiply that transformation. So our approach needs to honor the whole discipleship journey, not just the starting line. Evangelism and discipleship are not two separate tasks, run by two separate teams. They are two sides of the same coin—a single, ongoing process of walking with people toward Jesus.

> *We're not simply trying to save souls; we're trying to make disciples who embody and multiply transformation.*

The urgency of understanding this *why* is clear when we look at the current state of evangelism. A study by the Barna Group found that 47 percent of millennial Christians believe it is wrong to share their faith with the intent of converting someone. No wonder evangelism feels like a dying practice.[3]

This evangelistic hesitance is rooted in a deeper crisis of authenticity. Too often, when Christians engage culture, they prioritize spectacle and performance—using high-production worship, charismatic celebrity pastors, and emotion-driven events—over authenticity, genuine relationships, and a deep spirituality. As Christian philosopher and author Dallas Willard stated, "When you find problems in the church ... it is always a lack of discipleship that led to it."[4]

For many churches today, the Great Commission has quietly shifted into something else: an unspoken call to produce more Sunday spectators, plug them into a small group, and get them to serve once in a while. Yet, Scripture reveals a deeper mission—one centered on relational evangelism.

So how did we get here? How did we end up with two separate buckets—one for discipleship and one for evangelism?

Some of it comes from church culture. Over time, many churches have built systems that separate the two. There are programs to grow the people *inside* the church and events to reach those *outside*. One is for insiders; the other is for outreach. But this divide doesn't reflect the way of Jesus. Others trace the split to theology: One camp focuses on personal transformation (discipleship), and the other on transforming the world (evangelism). But this, too, is a false choice. Jesus did both. He formed people and sent them. He changed hearts and communities. He called people to follow him—and then told them to go out and love the world.

What we need isn't better programs for each category. We need a shift in perspective. Discipleship and evangelism are not separate tasks. They're inseparable aspects of the Great Commission. Both are about walking with people as they move toward Jesus—some may already be following, some may just be curious, but everyone's on a journey.

The How of Evangelship

The truth is, we don't have to choose between evangelizing *or* discipling. In real life, it's usually both at once. You're helping your neighbor fix their fence, and along the way they ask about your church. You're mentoring a younger coworker, and eventually they ask why your faith shapes how you lead. That's the overlap. That's where the walls come down and the gospel becomes visible.

This integrated life isn't neat or predictable. It's slow. It requires presence. It asks us to live what we believe—and to be available when someone else wants to learn more. It's not about having all the answers but being willing to walk alongside someone else as you both grow.

Jesus never told his disciples to "go convert people and then plug them into a class." He said, "Make disciples." That means teaching, yes—but also showing, walking, waiting, and loving. And it starts not with a program but with a relationship.

If we can recover this integrated vision—where evangelism and discipleship aren't two separate events but one ongoing process—we'll be able to meet people where they are and walk

> *The mission of the church isn't just to make converts or run programs—it's to make disciples who make disciples. And that kind of work doesn't happen in isolated moments. It happens over time, through relationship, in community, by grace.*

with them toward Jesus in ways that are both meaningful and sustainable.

Because in the end, the mission of the church isn't just to make converts or run programs—it's to make disciples who make disciples. And that kind of work doesn't happen in isolated moments. It happens over time, through relationship, in community, by grace.

Healthy discipleship and evangelism can only happen in the context of community. Jesus modeled this principle by forming deep relationships with twelve disciples, teaching and guiding them to spread the gospel. He prioritized deep, personal discipleship. As author and professor Robert Coleman observed, "Jesus devoted himself primarily to a few men, rather than the masses, so that the masses could at last be saved."[5]

For three years, Jesus lived with his twelve disciples, sharing meals and training them intimately so they could eventually multiply his message. This replication is key. In his dissertation, "Making Disciples of Jesus Christ," Jeffrey Howell Lynn notes, "When Jesus said, 'make disciples,' the disciples understood it to mean more than simply getting someone to believe in Jesus; they interpreted it as making others into what Jesus had made of them."[6]

This holistic, relational approach is at the heart of evangelship. And it culminated in the Great Commission, where Jesus gave them their mission:

> All authority in heaven and on earth has been given to me.
> Therefore go and make disciples of all nations, baptizing them
> in the name of the Father and of the Son and of the Holy Spirit,
> and teaching them to obey everything I have commanded you.
> And surely I am with you always, to the very end of the age.
>
> MATTHEW 28:18–20

Jesus emphasized a pattern: Start locally, then expand outward. This strategy was both a command—"But you will receive power when the Holy Spirit comes on you; and you will be my witnesses in Jerusalem, and in all Judea and Samaria, and to the ends of the earth" (Acts 1:8)—and a model, mirroring his own ministry, which began in his local community of Galilee before widening to reach others (Mark 1:39). By establishing a discipleship framework grounded in this teaching, we can reshape Western Christian culture to view evangelism as an organic extension of discipleship rather than an isolated event.

This is the approach Jesus modeled in his encounter with the Samaritan woman (John 4:4–26). Breaking cultural norms, he engaged her in conversation, revealing his identity as the Messiah. Rather than condemning her, he invited her into transformation and stayed in her town for two more days (John 4:40), reinforcing that discipleship requires investment and relationship. She, in turn, became a witness, leading the townspeople to "believe in [Jesus] because of the woman's testimony" (John 4:39).

The Great Commission as a Way of Life

This is the essence of evangelship—walking alongside people, sharing the gospel through relationship, and equipping them to do the same. The Great Commission is not about an event but a way of life. By embracing an "as you go" discipleship model—one woven into daily interactions and intentional relationships—we can reignite evangelism for generations to come.

A culture of discipleship naturally enhances evangelism. When individuals internalize the teachings and character of Jesus in their daily lives, transformation follows. This transformation compels believers to disciple others, including those outside the church. As new disciples grow in faith, they, too, become equipped to disciple others, creating a continuous cycle of spiritual growth and evangelism. This approach fosters a model of discipleship that inspires the next generation, even in a post-Christian society.

Evangelship is a bold strategy that propels Christians toward

---

Discipleship is ultimately about learning to live like Jesus—in real life, with real people, over time.

---

living out the Great Commission in their everyday interactions. As missiologist Alan Hirsch says,

> If the Great Commission is about discipleship, then discipleship should always be a major aspect in our thinking and approach to church vitality and mission. How can it not be? Just obey the Great Commission, and it will go well. It's all about discipleship from beginning to end.[7]

For many, discipleship brings to mind a small group, a class, or a mentorship program. Those things can be good and helpful. But discipleship is ultimately about learning to live like Jesus—in real life, with real people, over time. It's not about getting a spiritual education; it's about letting our whole lives be shaped by a relationship with Christ and inviting others into that journey with us.

The early church didn't have sign-up sheets for "Discipleship 101." They had shared lives. Jesus didn't run classes. He said, "Follow me," and then walked with people. He didn't just give instructions; he modeled a way of life. And those who followed him learned not just what to believe but also how to live. Discipleship is both personal and relational. It's about being transformed, yes—but also about being present with others as they are transformed, too. It's not about reaching a finish line of spiritual maturity before we start helping others. In fact, it's often in walking with others that we grow most.

Likewise, evangelism has often been reduced to a moment—a speech, a tract, a raised hand in a service. But real evangelism, the kind we see in the life of Jesus, is relational. It's not about pressure; it's about presence. It's not a script; it's a conversation.

Sharing the good news of Jesus doesn't just happen in pulpits or on stages. It happens over coffee, in text threads, during a walk, or through showing up consistently in someone's life. Evangelism isn't just proclamation—it's invitation. It's about helping people see where God is already at work in their story.

When we treat evangelism like a onetime event, we miss the slow work of God in people's hearts. We get impatient. We want decisions. But people aren't projects, and faith doesn't always come quickly. Sometimes, the best kind of evangelism is just sticking around long enough to help someone recognize that God's already been walking with them for a while.

Evangelship isn't just a new strategy; it's a return to the basic rhythm of Christian life. It's the church learning to breathe again. Slowly. Steadily. Naturally.

Because breathing isn't dramatic. It's not flashy. It's essential.

You don't need a microphone to do it. You don't need a big platform. You just need lungs. You just need life.

So, as you consider what it means to walk in the way of Jesus—to follow him, and to help others follow him—don't overcomplicate it. Just start with the breath.

Inhale the presence of God.

Exhale the love of God.

Repeat.

And in that rhythm, you'll find your purpose.

In that rhythm, you'll find your people.

In that rhythm, you'll find that the church is still alive—because it's still breathing.

Let's not forget how.

· ·

Reflection and Intention
Chapter Summary: Finding the Rhythm of Evangelship

- *Inhale, exhale* is the foundational idea of *evangelship*—the seamless integration of *evangelism and discipleship* as a relational lifestyle, not merely two disconnected church programs. Just as we need both *inhaling* and *exhaling* to live, the church must learn to balance *discipleship (inhale)* and *evangelism (exhale)* to truly thrive.

- The biblical foundation is traced back to Genesis 12, where Abraham is chosen—not to hoard blessing, but to be a *conduit of blessing to others*. This blessing-through-you principle continues through Jesus, the ultimate fulfillment of God's mission, and into the Great Commission, which is more than outreach—it's about a lifestyle of making *disciples who make disciples*.

- Jesus didn't split discipleship and evangelism into separate categories. He *walked with people*, loved them, taught them, and then *sent them*—not as events or programs, but as an organic, communal way of life. The early church lived this way, and we're invited to return to that rhythm.

- Evangelship is the church learning to *breathe again*. Not in a rush. Not in a performance. But in the quiet, powerful rhythm of love lived out loud.

Reflection Questions: A Personal Assessment
Take a few quiet moments to reflect on these questions. Write your thoughts down. Be honest with yourself and God.

- Which do you lean toward more—discipleship (inhale) or evangelism (exhale)? Why?
- Have you ever tried to "do ministry" while spiritually running on empty? What did that feel like?
- In what ways might your current church culture separate evangelism and discipleship? How could that be reshaped?
- Are you more likely to view evangelism as an event or a relationship? Why does that matter?
- What's one way you can begin to integrate discipleship and evangelism in your own life this week—not as a task but as a rhythm?

Breath Prayer

As you move forward, pause to say this simple breath prayer throughout your day:

> **Inhale:** *Lord, fill me with your presence.*
> **Exhale:** *Let me be a blessing to others.*

2

ignite heart-level transformation

Truly, the best thing any of us have to bring to leadership is our own transforming selves.

Ruth Haley Barton

LET ME TELL you about a guy I once met—we'll call him Mark. He had the Bible memorized in multiple translations. He could explain dispensationalism and walk you through the timeline of Revelation backwards. You know the type.

But when it came to real life? He had no grace for his coworkers. No joy in worship. No passion for the lost. One day, someone asked him a basic question about how God had transformed his life, and he froze. Not because he didn't know theology—but because he hadn't lived it.

Mark was a walking, talking Bible encyclopedia … but he'd never been discipled. He had information, not transformation.

Ultimately, the most powerful message we can offer the world isn't our words; it's the testimony of our own transformed life.

That's what this chapter—and this whole movement of evangelship—is about: moving from the head to the heart, from imitation to manifestation, from *knowing about Jesus* to *becoming like him* so others can see him through us.

You can master theology. Quote Calvin, Piper, or even the Hebrew word for "lovingkindness." You might lead the best small group or even help a hundred people get Bible-smart—and still not be helping anyone become like Jesus.

You can master theology. Quote Calvin, Piper, or even the Hebrew word for "lovingkindness." You might lead the best small group or even help a hundred people get Bible-smart—and still not be helping anyone become like Jesus.

Author, blogger, and speaker Frank Viola once said, "It's easy to get an A in Bible study but flunk Jesus."[1]

Let's sit with that for a second.

That quote from Frank Viola haunts me—in the best kind of way. Because it's true. And I think deep down, we all know it.

We've built a culture in the church that values the articulate over the authentic. We've settled for intellectual downloads over spiritual transformation. But the gospel Jesus brought wasn't a classroom lecture. It was an invitation: "Follow me."

Not Smarter Sinners, but Transformed Saints

Paul said in Romans 8:29 that God's goal for us is to be conformed to the image of his Son. Not just admire Jesus. Not just imitate his teachings. But to be transformed from the inside out into his likeness.

If the aim of discipleship is only knowledge, we're just building spiritual libraries. But if it's transformation, then we're building living temples—places where Christ dwells and is revealed.

Jesus never said, "By this everyone will know you are my disciples, if you can pass a Bible quiz." He said everyone will know we're his disciples "if [we] love one another" (John 13:35).

And that kind of love—the Galatians 5 kind of fruit—comes not from the intellect, but from intimacy with the Spirit: "Head knowledge without heart change is spiritual deception" (James 1:22, my paraphrase).

We've confused knowing about Jesus with knowing him. It's like knowing everything about a person's dating profile—but never going on the date.

From the Lecture Hall to the Living Room

When Paul was writing to the church in Thessalonica, he didn't say, "We loved you so much we created a discipleship class for you." He said, "We share[d] with you not only the gospel of God, but our own lives as well" (1 Thessalonians 2:8).

Real evangelship is relational, not just educational. It's life-on-life, not just lecture-on-lecture.

I'll never forget the men God placed in my life to disciple me. That's right—I had the rare privilege of being shaped by more than one spiritual father. While I've been influenced by many, there are five men in particular who left a permanent mark on my life. Perhaps God gave me these spiritual fathers to fill the void left by the absence of my biological father for much of my life.

> *Real evangelship is relational, not just educational. It's life-on-life, not just lecture-on-lecture.*

Let me introduce them to you:

- Rev. William Vazquez, my senior pastor, taught me what it means to be a spiritual father.

- Rev. Antonio Plá showed me the heart of a true shepherd.
- Rev. Dr. Raúl Marrero poured into me lessons on life and fatherhood. Though he, Pastor Pla, and Pastor Vazquez are now home with the Lord, their love and teachings still echo within me.
- Rev. Dr. Wilfredo "Choco" De Jesús modeled integrity, leadership, and the weighty importance of obeying God.
- Rev. Peter Avilés, the one I now call "Dad," has mentored me deeply—shaping my theology, sharpening my preaching, and showing me what it means to be a man of God.

These men discipled me in real life—not in classrooms but in restaurants, during hospital visits and late-night coffee runs, and in the middle of heartbreaks and dark seasons. They didn't hand me a twelve-step program. They handed me their lives.

And somewhere in the raw, unscripted moments of relationship, I not only found Jesus—I saw him. In their wounds, their witness, and their walk, I learned what true discipleship looks like.

That's when it clicked: You can't disciple from a distance. Jesus didn't disciple from the clouds—he came close, ate fish with sinners, cried at funerals, walked dusty roads, and put his hands on lepers.

"Discipleship," Dallas Willard once said, "is the process of becoming who Jesus would be if He were you."[2] And you can't do that from behind a pulpit alone. You have to open your life, not just your Bible.

There's this verse in 2 Corinthians 3:3 that says we're like letters—written not with ink but with the Spirit of the living God, not on stone tablets but on human hearts.

That's deep. And it reminds us that if we're only teaching to people's heads, we're only scratching the surface. True evangelship targets the spirit. It ministers to the heart—the place where real change happens.

Fire Alone Is Not Enough

Let's talk about something most Christians won't admit out loud: We're tired.

And not just physically—we're spiritually tired. Passionate about reaching people but secretly wondering if we're still anchored ourselves. On fire for the mission but emotionally fried. Discipling others but barely hanging on ourselves.

I've been there. Maybe you have, too.

It's what happens when we confuse momentum for maturity … or when we value depth without direction.

There's something powerful about zeal. That "let's-go-change-the-world" energy. That Holy-Spirit-breathing-on-your-neck kind of boldness.

And it's beautiful—until it's not.

Because without spiritual formation—without roots—you'll burn out trying to save people you were never meant to carry.

You'll mistake urgency for intimacy. And you'll run hard … but not necessarily *with* Jesus.

Evangelship without formation is like building a fire with dry leaves. It sparks quickly … but it doesn't last. If evangelship is going to last, we need both the *fire* of mission and the *form* of formation. Not either/or. But both/and.

Formation Alone Is Not Enough Either

Now flip it.

Some people are deep. They practice silence and solitude. They read thick books. They could teach a class on contemplative prayer. But their faith is all roots with no branches. All inward with no outward. That's not how Jesus lived. He went to the mountain to pray—and then came down to heal, teach, and eat with sinners. The closer you are to Jesus, the more you love the people he loves. Spiritual formation that never overflows into mission is incomplete. It's like a fireplace with no flame—structured, but cold.

> **The closer you are to Jesus, the more you love the people he loves.**

Jesus Had Both: The Fire and the Form

Let's just look at Jesus for a moment.

- He healed crowds … and then disappeared to pray.
- He confronted injustice … and withdrew to solitude.
- He discipled twelve … and made time for the one.
- He lived with urgency … and moved with unhurried presence.
- He was on fire … and he was formed.

> **Jesus didn't come to burn out in three years. He came to burn bright for eternity.**

And that's our model. Jesus didn't just *do* ministry—he ministered *from intimacy*. Jesus didn't come to burn out in three years. He came to burn bright for eternity.

The Rhythm of Fire and Form

Let me share something I learned the hard way.

There was a season in my life where I was *doing all the things*—preaching, discipling, leading, multiplying, missioning. But I was empty inside.

I was on fire … but I was burning out.

Until one mentor looked me in the eye and said, "You're not the church's savior; Jesus is, and you are not Jesus!"

Oof.

So I paused. I unplugged. I relearned how to sit with Jesus—not to prep a sermon, not to disciple someone—but just to *be* with him.

And slowly, the fire came back. But this time, it was grounded in something deeper. Something durable.

Here's the good news: Fire and form aren't enemies. They're dance partners. One fuels the other. So how do we live in that rhythm?

Spend daily time with Jesus. Not as a box to check—but as the oxygen your fire needs. "If you remain in me and I in you, you will bear much fruit; apart from me you can do nothing" (John 15:5). No fruit. No fire. No formation—without *remaining*. Even fifteen minutes of honest, present prayer can ground you more than a twelve-hour ministry day.

Live from identity, not activity. Your worth isn't based on your performance. You're a beloved son or daughter first. Fire says, "Go." Formation says, "You're already loved." You need both. Before Jesus did a single miracle, the Father said: "This is my Son, whom I love" (Matthew 3:17). Don't forget that.

Use mission to stretch you. Fire isn't the enemy of formation—it's the gym where formation gets tested. Discipling someone will show you how impatient you are. Sharing Jesus will expose your fears. Opening your home will reveal your pride. That's not failure. That's formation. Let mission form you. And let formation fuel your mission.

Reflection and Intention
Chapter Summary: Igniting Heart-Level Transformation

- Evangelship is *transformation, not just information*; knowledge without lived faith leaves people untransformed.
- True discipleship moves *from the head to the heart,* from theory to incarnation, from imitation to manifestation.
- Spiritual growth happens *relationally,* not merely academically; life-on-life discipleship shapes more than classroom teaching ever could.
- *Fire without formation burns out; formation without fire goes cold.* The rhythm of evangelship requires both zeal for mission and rootedness in Christ.
- *Daily practices* like abiding in Christ, living from identity, and letting mission stretch you keep the *fire and form in balance.*

Reflection Questions: A Personal Assessment
Take a few quiet moments to reflect on these questions. Write your thoughts down. Be honest with yourself and God.

- Do you know *about* Jesus, or do you truly know him in a way that transforms your heart and your actions?
- Where in your life are you prioritizing knowledge over relationship, or activity over intimacy with God?
- Who around you needs presence more than instruction? How can you show up incarnationally?
- Which spiritual practices help you stay rooted, so your zeal doesn't burn out?

- How are you modeling Christ in both the ordinary and messy parts of your life?
- Are you using your mission to stretch and shape you, or are you trying to carry it in your own strength?

Breath Prayer

As you move forward, pause to say this simple breath prayer throughout your day:

Inhale: *Jesus, shape my heart and fill my life with you.*
Exhale: *Let my life reflect your love and power to others.*

3

live questionably

Live in such a way that your life would not make sense if God did not exist.

Tim Chester

LET'S TALK ABOUT weird Christians. Not the cringey kind—shouting on corners, holding signs, or trying to argue strangers into the kingdom. I mean weird Christians in the best possible way. The beautiful, *unexplainable*, question-provoking kind.

You've probably met one.

The single mom who gives generously, even when her bank account is in the red.

The guy who forgives someone who publicly humiliated him—*with joy*.

The couple who opens their tiny home week after week to welcome their neighborhood.

The woman in your office who always speaks peace and never gossips, even when everyone else is chewing someone up behind their back.

There's something about them you can't quite put your finger on.

That's the power of living questionably—when your life creates curiosity. When people see something in you that feels *otherworldly*. It's the natural overflow of what we talked about in the previous chapter—a life transformed by God.

The Early Church Didn't Have a Platform—They Had a Presence

Here's something wild: The early church didn't have TikTok, pulpits, podcasts, or publishing deals. They didn't have Christian bookstores or celebrity pastors. Yet the gospel spread like wildfire.

How?

Their lives didn't just reflect Jesus—they provoked questions about him.

Sociologist Rodney Stark observes that the explosive growth of the early church didn't expand through mass crusades or political power but through everyday lives of compassion that set believers apart from their world. Christianity's strength, he explains, wasn't found merely in its promise of heaven but in the radically different way its followers lived—creating communities of charity, belonging, and hope that revitalized the cities of the Roman Empire.[1]

The early church was filled with ordinary people living such countercultural lives that the Roman world took notice.

They didn't just teach about Jesus. They manifested him—in their homes, businesses, marriages, sufferings, and celebrations.

Peter gives us a simple blueprint in 1 Peter 3:15: "Always be prepared to give an answer to everyone who asks you to give the reason for the hope that you have."

But don't miss the built-in assumption: Someone's *asking*.

You're living in such a way—so full of hope, peace, kindness, joy, generosity, forgiveness—that someone finally leans in and goes, "Okay, what's your deal?"

That's the secret sauce of evangelship. It's not just proclamation—it's incarnation.

It's a lifestyle that begs a question. And when that question comes, the gospel has a wide-open door. Australian missiologist and theologian Michael Frost emphasizes that evangelism flows naturally when our lives are so compelling that others are drawn to follow the God we serve.[2]

A truly transformed life provokes curiosity and conversation in three magnetic ways, echoing the witness of the early church.

Curiosity: Living with Joy That Defies Circumstance

The first believers often demonstrated radical peace and even joy while being imprisoned, persecuted, or facing martyrdom. Paul and Silas sang songs in prison after a beating (Acts 16:25). Stephen did not cry in fear or pain as he was being stoned (Acts 7:54–60); his final act was a prayer of forgiveness for his killers (v.60). And after being arrested, flogged, and commanded not to speak about Jesus, the apostles left the Sanhedrin, rejoicing that they'd been counted worthy to suffer dishonor for Jesus' name (Acts 5:40–41). This unshakable hope in the face of suffering was a mystery the Roman world could not explain.

In today's anxious society, a Christian who handles financial strain, betrayal, or illness with unshakable peace and quiet joy is questionable. People don't ask questions when we blend in; they ask when our reaction to suffering stands out.

> *People don't ask questions when we blend in; they ask when our reaction to suffering stands out.*

Compassion: Loving When It Costs You

Early Christians stayed in plague-ridden cities to care for the dying while others fled. They adopted discarded Roman babies and welcomed the sick, the poor, and the outsider.[3]

Today, this radical love means prioritizing the marginalized, extending unconditional forgiveness, and practicing costly generosity to people who can't repay us. Acts of radical love aren't just nice—they are *scandalous*.

Countercultural Community: Becoming the Alternative Society

The church wasn't just a service—it was a new family where social barriers were obliterated. Rich and poor ate together (1 Corinthians 11:20–22). Jews and Gentiles shared life (Galatians 3:28). Men and women ministered alongside each other (Romans 16:1–4). They became, in the words of Presbyterian pastor and scholar Eugene Peterson, "a colony of heaven in the country of death."[4]

Today, this means allowing our church communities to be places of welcome that defy cultural divides—where people of different political views, socioeconomic classes, and races genuinely share life and minister together. Our unity shows what it means to be an alternative society in a broken world.

Trunk Talk

Back in my college days, one of the coolest jobs I landed was working at the Chicago White Sox stadium, right up in the skyboxes with the Levy organization. Now, for a die-hard White Sox fan, this was a dream gig. I got to be around the game I loved, and the cherry on top? A bunch of my buddies worked there, too. It felt like we had the best of both worlds: making money and hanging out while doing it.

But the job wasn't all peanuts and Cracker Jack. The tough part came after the games. Since we worked the skyboxes, we had to clean up and reset everything—sometimes late into the night. And when the Sox went into extra innings, like they did one night, things got really late. I'm talking 1:30 in the morning late. Now, if you know anything about 35th and Shields, you know it wasn't exactly the safest place to be wandering around at that hour. We were just a bunch of college kids trying to get home, but only one of us had a car—and that car fit five. There were seven of us. You do the math.

That meant two of us were out of luck and would have to make the long walk to the Brown Line ... through a neighborhood that wasn't too friendly after dark.

So one of my friends—probably half-joking—said, "Hey, if you want a ride, two of you can squeeze into the trunk."

Now, let me pause and say: I do not recommend this. And yeah, it wasn't my brightest decision either. But then again, how many teenagers are known for making wise decisions?

So there I was, in the trunk of a car, with another guy, hoping we'd make it home in one piece. It was dark. Cramped. Hot. And very illegal. But somewhere in the middle of all that, something unexpected happened.

My friend—yeah, the one stuffed in the trunk with me— turned and said, "Larry, can I ask you something? You don't drink like the other guys. You don't talk like them either. You're just ... different. Aren't you even scared right now?"

I paused for a second. Honestly, I was scared. Somewhere in the back of my mind, I could hear my mom's voice screaming, *"Mijo, what are you thinking?!"*

But I looked at him and said, "Nah, I'm not scared. I have Jesus in my heart. I know I'm saved. I know where I'm going. And that makes it a lot easier to handle what's happening right now."

He was quiet for a moment. Then he said something I'll never forget: "I want that confidence, too. I don't even know what would happen to me if something went wrong. I don't know about my future."

Right there—in the dark, cramped, barely breathable space of that trunk—I got to share the love of Jesus. I didn't preach a sermon. I didn't have a Bible open. I just lived out who I was, and it sparked a question. That question opened a door. That door led to a prayer. And in that unexpected place, he gave his life to Christ.

After that, he started going to church with me. Eventually, he got married, moved to Atlanta, and to this day, he still loves Jesus.

Here's what I've learned: Sometimes the most powerful witness isn't the words we rehearse—it's the life we live when no one's looking. Or, in my case, when someone's watching you in the trunk of a car.

Evangelship isn't just about proclaiming—it's about provoking. It's about living a life so rooted in Jesus that it causes others to pause and ask, "Why are you like that?" It's not always about having persuasive arguments. Sometimes it's just about having a presence that reflects peace, a confidence that radiates hope, and a love that shines in dark places.

> *When we live questionably, our lives become the sermon.*

When we live questionably, our lives become the sermon. And the people around us? They become curious. And in their curiosity, God begins to stir their hearts toward life change.

So let me ask you: Is your life stirring up questions?

Jesus' Questionable Life

If there was ever someone who embodied the art of living a life that stirred curiosity, conviction, and conversation, it was Jesus.

Jesus didn't just show up and preach sermons; he lived in a way that disrupted the norms of his day. His life stirred up questions at every turn. The way he moved, spoke, healed, and welcomed people made others stop and ask, "Who is this man?"

His ministry constantly defied expectations.

He ate with tax collectors and sinners (Luke 5:29–32).

He touched lepers and healed them (Mark 1:40–45).

He spoke with a Samaritan woman at a well, breaking ethnic, gender, and religious barriers (John 4:7–26).

He welcomed children, even when the disciples tried to push them away (Mark 10:13–16).

He remained silent before Pilate, though he had every right to defend himself (Matthew 27:12–14).

He flipped over tables in the temple out of righteous anger (Matthew 21:12–13).

Jesus lived in such a way that people couldn't ignore him. Even his enemies were perplexed. His actions sparked confusion and awe—leading many to ask, "By what authority are you doing these things?" (Mark 11:28).

Studying the life of Jesus reveals how magnetic, intriguing, and constructively disruptive he was—a life that naturally provoked questions from those around him.

This was true even in his death. When Jesus breathed his last on the cross, the Roman centurion—a man trained for violence, not wonder—looked up and declared, "Surely this man was the Son of God!" (Mark 15:39). Why? Because even in death, Jesus lived questionably.

> *Even in death, Jesus lived questionably.*

If we are to be his disciples, our lives must echo his—lived in such a way that others are compelled to ask, "Why are you different?"

Michael Frost reinforces this exact idea in *Surprise the World* when he describes the type of life that evokes these questions: "We need to become a godly, intriguing, socially adventurous, joyous presence in the lives of others."[5] This happens by consistently living out missional habits that demonstrate the reign of God in our lives. As Frost goes on to say, this is why "those of us who are not gifted evangelists need to foster habits in our lives that draw us out into the lives of unbelievers and invite the kinds of questions that lead to evangelistic sharing. When our lives become questionable, our neighbors invite us to proclaim the reign of God."[6]

Paul captured this in Colossians 4:5–6: "Be wise in the way you act toward outsiders; make the most of every opportunity. Let your conversation be always full of grace, seasoned with salt, so that you may know how to answer everyone."

Tell the Real Story

When that question comes—when someone asks "Why?"—that's your open door. That's your "trunk moment." That's the Holy Spirit stirring curiosity.

People don't need rehearsed speeches. They need real stories.

Your testimony—how God has moved in your life—is one of the most powerful things you have. And here's the good news: You don't need to have a dramatic "I was a mess, then Jesus saved me" story for it to matter.

Maybe your story isn't about a radical transformation. Maybe it's about quiet faithfulness, about how God has been with you through ordinary days, heartbreak, doubts, and joy. That story matters, too.

The key is to be real. People can tell when you're putting on a show. They don't need perfection; they need authenticity.

Share your struggles. Share your doubts. Share the moments when you felt like God wasn't there—and then how you saw him show up. That's what connects. That's what resonates.

At the end of the day, people will believe your faith is real, not because you say all the right words, but because you live in a way that backs them up.

You don't have to be the loudest person in the room. You just have to be authentic.

When you're kind when others are cruel, people notice.

When you serve without expecting anything in return, people notice.

When you hold on to hope in the middle of suffering, people notice.

And when they ask why you are the way you are, you get to tell them.

Live What You Believe

We've often been taught the gospel primarily as a message to be communicated verbally—a presentation to be shared. And there's a time and a place for that. But living questionably is about demonstrating these truths, moving them from theory to practice. Below is a simple breakdown of the key points of the gospel: Creation, Fall, Rescue, Response, and Restoration. This is followed by everyday ways we can actively live out and embody those truths—not through pressure or performance but through authentic presence and love.

Creation

The Gospel Story: Designed with Purpose

- God created the world and humanity with intentionality, beauty, and goodness.
- Every person is made in the image of God (Genesis 1:27), designed for relationship with him and with one another.

The Gospel Lived Out: Honor Everyone's Worth

- Treat others with dignity, regardless of status or belief.
- Celebrate beauty and creativity—in people, art, nature, and culture.
- Speak life into people, especially those who feel unseen or dismissed.

Fall

The Gospel Story: Sin Broke Everything

- Humanity chose independence from God (Genesis 3), leading to brokenness—spiritual separation, relational pain, injustice, and death.
- Every person experiences the effects of this brokenness and cannot fix it on their own (Romans 3:23–24).

The Gospel Lived Out: Practice Humility and Compassion

- Acknowledge your own flaws and extend grace to others.
- Be quick to listen, slow to judge.
- Sit with people in their mess without needing to fix them.

Rescue

The Gospel Story: Jesus Entered Our Mess

- God didn't leave us in our brokenness. He sent Jesus—fully God and fully human—to live a sinless life, die on the cross, and rise again (John 3:16).
- Jesus took the penalty for sin and made a way for people to be restored to God.

The Gospel Lived Out: Be Open About Hope

- When the moment is right, share how Jesus has changed you—your peace, your purpose, your healing.
- Pray for others and let them know you're doing it.
- Show forgiveness, generosity, and love that doesn't make sense by worldly standards.

Response

The Gospel Story: An Invitation to Follow

- The gospel is not just information—it's an invitation.
- Through faith and repentance, anyone can be forgiven, restored, and made new (Romans 10:9).
- Following Jesus is a lifelong journey of becoming more like him.

The Gospel Lived Out: Live a Life of Invitation

- Invite people into your life: meals, coffee, community. Let them see your faith in action.
- Be available for spiritual conversations—answering questions without pressure.
- Let people know they don't have to have it all together to come to Jesus (because you don't either).

Restoration

The Gospel Story: Joining God's Mission

- The gospel doesn't end at personal salvation. Jesus is making all things new—spiritually, socially, environmentally, and relationally (Revelation 21:5).
- Christians are called to join that mission—living as agents of reconciliation, healing, and justice in the world.

The Gospel Lived Out: Work Toward Wholeness

- Serve your community. Volunteer. Support what brings healing.
- Advocate for justice. Be a peacemaker.
- Model hope in a cynical world—because you believe a better world is coming.

> *Evangelship is about letting the gospel shape your everyday life in ways that provoke questions and that people can see, feel, and trust.*

Living with Intentional Distinction

Evangelship is about letting the gospel shape your everyday life in ways that provoke questions and that people can see, feel, and trust.

There's a difference between being open about your faith and making people feel like they're being trapped in a sales pitch. Nobody likes that feeling—when a friendly conversation turns into a forced "Have you accepted Jesus as your personal Lord and Savior?" moment.

This isn't about manipulation. It's about honesty.

Be upfront about who you are. If Jesus is central to your life, don't hide it. You don't have to announce it with a megaphone, but you also shouldn't feel like you have to avoid mentioning him just to make people comfortable.

If your faith comes up naturally, talk about it. If someone asks about your weekend and you went to church, say that. If you're going through something hard and prayer is what's getting you through, share that.

The people around you should know you love Jesus—not because you shove it down their throats, but because it's woven into your life in a way that's undeniable.

The goal isn't to be undercover Christians.

Jesus didn't call his followers to a covert mission, sneaking around, hoping no one would notice their faith. He said, "You are the light of the world. A town built on a hill cannot be hidden" (Matthew 5:14). He never called us to blend in. He called us to be salt and light (Matthew 5:13–16)—to preserve, to shine, to be noticeably different.

So, if you love Jesus—let people know.

Jesus' actions made sense only in light of the kingdom he was proclaiming. Without that lens, he seemed strange, even offensive. But to those with eyes to see, his life was an invitation into something far greater.

A life of love, holiness, peace, joy, and conviction stands out in a world marked by chaos and compromise. It's a questionable life. As Paul says in Philippians 2:15, "Shine among them like stars in the sky, as you hold firmly to the word of life."

So live courageously. Live joyfully. Live peacefully. Live generously. Live truthfully. Live questionably.

And when the questions come—point them straight to Jesus.

. . . .

Reflection and Intention
Chapter Summary: Living Questionably

- Evangelship begins *not with louder words* but with a *distinctive life* that provokes questions.

- Being upfront about who you are means *weaving your faith into everyday conversations* and choices without pressure or performance.

- Your testimony—whether dramatic or ordinary—is powerful because it's real. *Authenticity always resonates more than polish.*

- A questionable life is one that *radiates joy* in suffering, *compassion* that costs, and *community* that defies cultural divides.

- The gospel story (Creation, Fall, Rescue, Response, Restoration) *isn't just something to explain*—it's something to live, every day, through dignity, humility, hope, invitation, and redemption.

- Making your beliefs known is less about perfect words and more about *living with integrity* so people can see Jesus in you.

- Faith isn't a *sales pitch*—it's an *authentic way of life* that naturally *reveals Jesus.*

Reflection Questions: A Personal Assessment

Take some time with these. Let them probe your rhythms, habits, and witness.

- Does your life raise questions in others—or does it blend in so much that it feels unremarkable?
- When was the last time you shared something about Jesus naturally in conversation? How did that go?
- What part of your story could encourage someone right now—even if it feels small or ordinary?
- Which gospel theme (Creation, Fall, Rescue, Response, Restoration) feels most natural for you to live out—and which one challenges you the most?
- If someone shadowed you for a week, what would they see? Would anything about your choices, words, generosity, or peace point them to Jesus?
- Do you ever hide your faith to avoid awkwardness or rejection? Why?
- How can you be more intentional this week about letting your life—not just your words—point to Jesus?

Breath Prayer

As you move forward, pause to say this simple breath prayer throughout your day:

Inhale: *Jesus, make my life compelling.*
Exhale: *May every question point to you.*

4

don't discount yourself

We do a great disservice to the church when we convey the impression that the gift of the Spirit is reserved for some kind of spiritual aristocracy, clergy or missionaries, but not the rank and file. The gift of the Spirit is the birthright of every believer.

John Stott

THROUGHOUT HISTORY, GOD has consistently chosen the most unlikely individuals to carry out his work. The Bible is full of stories about God using ordinary people in extraordinary ways. Moses had a speech impediment, yet God called him to confront Pharaoh and lead the Israelites out of Egypt (Exodus 4:10–12). Mary, a young, seemingly ordinary woman, was chosen to bear the Son of God (Luke 1:26–38). The disciples were fishermen, tax collectors, and everyday workers, yet Jesus entrusted them with the gospel message that would change the world. At Pentecost (Acts 2), God empowered these ordinary men to continue the work of Jesus and carry out the Great Commission. As a direct result, "the Lord added to their number daily those who were being saved" (Acts 2:47).

Before we move on to explore the practical ways we live out an evangelship lifestyle, we must address the one thing most of us feel, even if we never admit it out loud: We don't feel qualified or good enough.

We look at the Great Commission and immediately look at ourselves, seeing all the gaps, mistakes, and inexperience. The nagging doubts whisper: *I don't know enough Scripture. I'm too broken. I'll say the wrong thing. That's the job for professionals.* But discipleship isn't about being perfect or how much you know—it's about how much you love. If you have Christ's love inside you, you already have everything you need to be a disciple-maker.

> *If you have Christ's love inside you, you already have everything you need to be a disciple-maker.*

Blessing over Conversion

The reason many of us feel unqualified is that we think evangelism requires a stage and a script. We think we have to stand up, know all the answers, and impose our beliefs on people. When we think this way, we forget that we are carriers of good news and of blessing.

In today's culture, relationships matter more than ever. Thankfully, the days of cold-call evangelism and forced conversions are fading, making way for a more relational, person-centered approach. Dr. Rick Richardson, professor of evangelism at Wheaton College, observes, "In this kind of culture, the ancient vision of blessing others often resonates with people."[1]

This is more aligned with God's plan throughout history. In an earlier chapter, we talked about how God's mission to redeem the world has always been about blessing, beginning with his covenant with Abraham: "I will bless you ... and all peoples on earth will be blessed through you" (Genesis 12:2–3). We are blessed to be a blessing.

A study by Dr. Mark Russell, *Blessers vs. Converters*, explored two missionary approaches in Thailand: one focused on serving and blessing people, and the other on direct conversion efforts. The results were staggering. The missionaries who prioritized blessing saw ninety-six conversions, while those focused on conversion saw only two—a 48:1 ratio.[2]

The study underscores the power of relational evangelism. When we engage people with the intent to bless rather than convert, we create space for God to do his transformative work. Evangelism is not about closing a sale; it's about opening a relationship.

As research from Barna points out, we need to adopt the mentality that we are simply "guides and conduits through which a sovereign God does His work."[3] Rather than seeing evangelism as something we do *for* God, we must recognize that it is a process initiated by God working within us. The mission itself is a tool that God uses to shape both us and those we're discipling.

The B.L.E.S.S. Model for Everyday Evangelism

Dave and Jon Ferguson, brothers and cofounders of Community Christian Church, Chicago, developed the B.L.E.S.S. model as a practical framework for relational evangelism that blesses and serves:

- **B**—Begin with Prayer: Ask God to show you whom he wants you to bless.
- **L**—Listen: Take the time to hear people's stories without an agenda.

- **E**—Eat: Share meals and meaningful conversations.
- **S**—Serve: Meet real needs and love people where they are.
- **S**—Story: Share your faith journey naturally when the time is right.[4]

By living out these principles, evangelism shifts from a transactional event to a transformational lifestyle. We are not called to coerce or convince; we are called to love, serve, and walk alongside people on their journey toward Jesus. It's something any of us can do.

This is the invitation of evangelship: to shift our mindset from convincing to connecting, from pressuring to blessing. Jesus didn't command us to win arguments—he commanded us to love our neighbors. When we prioritize presence over persuasion, we embody the kind of gospel that draws people in instead of pushing them away. Blessing others is not a tactic—it's the heart of God's mission. And when we lead with prayer, listen with empathy, share meals, serve with sincerity, and tell our stories with humility, we become vessels of God's love in a world hungry for authenticity. Evangelism doesn't start with a script—it starts with a relationship.

You Don't Need a Title, Just a Yes

The truth is, you don't need to be a pastor or have a specific title to make a real difference. Scripture is clear: Every believer is called to participate in the Great Commission. We are all God's people in Christ, and we all share the responsibility to help others become followers of Jesus.

Church culture can often focus too much on attendance, big events, and professional leaders doing all the work. But real spiritual growth isn't just about counting numbers or big moments; it's about what's happening beneath the surface. It's about lives being changed and people growing closer to Jesus.

If we're going to see this kind of deep, lasting change, it means each of us playing our part in our everyday lives—at home, at work, and in our neighborhoods. This is evangelship: Every person matters, and every believer can help others follow Jesus in real, relational, and accessible ways.

When Jesus selected his twelve disciples, he didn't just call them to listen to his teachings; he called them to be sent ones (Luke 6:12–13)—people who would take his message out into the world.

To create a church culture where sharing our faith is a natural, everyday way of life, we all need to help others find and follow Jesus. We need to look beyond the walls of the sanctuary and see our whole lives as a mission field.

God Doesn't Call the Qualified

If you've ever felt unqualified to share your faith, look no further than the team Jesus originally assembled. He didn't go looking for spiritual all-stars. When he launched his ministry, Jesus didn't choose synagogue leaders, theologians, or religious celebrities to walk with him. He chose fishermen. A tax collector. A political zealot. Regular, working-class folks with calloused hands, short tempers, and very little in the way of formal religious education.

In fact, Acts 4:13 tells us that the religious leaders were shocked by the disciples' boldness because they were "unschooled, ordinary men." But that's the point. Jesus chose them *on purpose*. Not because they had it all together, but because they were teachable, hungry, and willing to follow. They didn't have impressive résumés—but they had open hearts.

This wasn't normal for the time. In first-century Jewish culture, rabbis typically handpicked the best and brightest—young men who had spent years studying the Torah and showed the most promise. You had to earn your place. But Jesus flipped that script.

Instead of waiting for the best candidates to come to him, he went out and found the ones no one else would've picked.

And here's what that tells us: Jesus' invitation isn't for the elite. It's for the willing. God's calling isn't about our qualifications—it's about the Holy Spirit's power working through us. It's about everyday believers stepping boldly into the extraordinary work of God's kingdom.

> *God doesn't call the equipped; he equips the called. And if you are in Christ, you are called.*

You don't need a seminary degree to disciple others. You don't need to have all the answers. You simply need to be willing. God doesn't call the equipped; he equips the called. And if you are in Christ, you are called.

Evangelship isn't about professionals leading the charge. Author and pastor Ed Stetzer once said, "When we specialize that which was called to be normal, we paralyze everyone else."[5] And wow … have we done that in the church. We've hired evangelists and outsourced discipleship. We've turned ministry into a spectator sport, and people are stuck on the sidelines, thinking, *That's not for me.*

But God doesn't ask for your specialization—he asks for your surrender.

God doesn't need your platform—he needs your yes.

Stop Hiding, Start Seeking

Let me take you back to something simple—something almost childlike.

Picture a frantic moment—police, parents, firefighters, even a helicopter overhead. Everyone is searching in panic. A boy is missing.

Eventually, the search ends.

And where was he?

Hiding quietly. Giggling. Thinking it was a game.

It's funny, but it's familiar. Not just because we've all played hide-and-seek, but because many of us are still playing it with God. We're hiding … and he's still seeking.

I loved playing hide-and-seek as a kid. Lights off. Heart pounding. Trying not to breathe too loudly. I play it now with my kids—and maybe one day with my grandkids. But the older I get, the more I realize the Bible is one long game of hide-and-seek. Only this time, the one doing the seeking is God.

He sought out Abraham. He called Moses from a burning bush. He whispered to Samuel in the night. He found Zacchaeus in a tree and met a woman at a well. Sometimes he does the seeking himself, and sometimes—like with Philip and the Ethiopian eunuch or Samuel looking for David—he invites us to join him.

But what happens when we refuse to be found? Or when we refuse to join the search?

Have we turned prayer into a hiding place instead of a launching pad? Have we mistaken sanctification for separation, isolating ourselves from the very people Jesus came to save? Have we convinced ourselves that we can simply wait on God and hide from the mission he is calling us to, isolating ourselves from the very people Jesus came to save?

Some of us are still waiting for a crisis to call us out of hiding—a blinding light, a burning bush, something dramatic. But you don't need to crash or hit rock bottom to come out of hiding. Most of God's

> *Most of God's invitations come quietly. In whispers. Nudges. Conversations. You just need to respond.*

invitations come quietly. In whispers. Nudges. Conversations. You just need to respond.

You can be lost in the house. That's what Jesus taught in the Parable of the Lost Coin (Luke 15:8–10). You can show up to church every week and still be hiding—behind shame, insecurity, fear that you're not enough. But Jesus is still speaking. And he's not just calling the Sauls—the dramatically broken and publicly renowned. He's calling the Ananiases—the ones who feel too ordinary, too unqualified, too unknown to be part of something extraordinary.

One Obedient Yes

Ananias was just a regular guy, a disciple likely hiding himself in fear of Saul (later known as Paul). Yet, God interrupted his hiding and invited him right into the middle of a miracle (Acts 9). Saul was blinded by a light, but he couldn't see until Ananias—an ordinary man of flesh and bone—laid hands on him. Ananias's quiet act of obedience made him the carrier of Saul's healing.

Ananias wasn't an apostle. He had no followers. But he had one thing: availability. When he heard the voice of God, his first response was "Yes, Lord"—a posture of someone ready to be sent, even before knowing the dangerous assignment waiting for him. Yet, when God told him to go to Saul, Ananias's humanity surfaced: "You mean *that* guy? The one who's been killing us?"

But God didn't explain. He just said, "Go. I've chosen him."

Evangelship is about saying yes to people we don't fully understand. Trusting God's plan when it doesn't make sense. Walking toward what feels risky or uncomfortable, believing that the story is bigger than what we can see. Ananias didn't heal Saul—God did. But Ananias *carried* the healing. He was the conduit. He laid his hands on Saul and called him "brother." And the scales fell from Saul's eyes.

Your voice matters like that. Your story matters like that. Someone needs what you carry. You're not just offering advice. You're unlocking purpose. You're not just preaching sermons. You're guiding people toward their God-given destiny.

Ananias was the spiritual coach Paul didn't know he needed. He helped him get back on his feet—literally and spiritually. This relational support is crucial because we can know a lot *about* Jesus and still miss him. What changes us isn't information. It's formation. And that happens through being willing to say yes, even when the outcome isn't clear.

Some of us are still waiting for the "right" time, the perfect moment, the official title. But it's clear that Ananias didn't wait to build a curriculum or start a ministry. He simply obeyed. That one act of faith opened the door to one of the most powerful apostolic movements in history. Thirteen books in your New Testament trace back to one obedient yes.

So what's at stake if you keep hiding?

Who misses their Damascus moment because your voice stayed silent?

We don't need more celebrities in the church. We need more Ananiases. Men and women who are willing to know the story— not just of Jesus, but of the people God has connected them to. People who apply the story, not as theory, but transformation. Who own it. Live it. Tell it. Because healing often travels through human voices.

Someone Needs What You Carry

That's why your frequency is needed. Erwin McManus, in his book *Seven Frequencies of Communication*, states that "Human communication at its core is about frequency. All of us speak at a unique frequency. We are all designed for not only communication but connection."[6] This means that God has somehow wired me to speak at a frequency that will connect more clearly with those who have the same frequency as me. Despite our proximity to others, "if we are speaking at the wrong frequency we will not be able to hear each other."[7]

And you—leader, pastor, preacher, disciple—possess a necessary voice that particular individuals need to hear.

The message needs a messenger. As Paul wrote,

> But how can people call for help if they don't know who to trust? And how can they know who to trust if they haven't heard of the One who can be trusted? And how can they hear if nobody tells them? And how is anyone going to tell them, unless someone is sent to do it?

ROMANS 10:14–15 MSG

When God needed someone to reach Saul, he didn't call Peter. He didn't send John. He didn't resurrect Stephen. He called Ananias, an unknown disciple. No title. No pulpit. No social media following. God didn't send a professional. He sent someone who was available and carried the right resonance for Saul's specific need.

Your life emits a divinely tuned frequency—a sound of redemption that someone is waiting to hear, and that only your journey, experience, and tone can deliver.

Here's what I've come to believe: Your life emits a divinely tuned frequency—a sound of redemption that someone is waiting to hear, and that only your journey, experience, and tone can deliver. Perhaps you are called to be an Ananias to a Saul—uniquely equipped to speak God's truth to a particular individual. And if you stay silent, they may stay lost.

Are you willing to be an Ananias? Today could be your turn to be found. Maybe you've been hiding behind excuses, doubts, shame, and fear. Maybe you've been waiting for a sign that you're ready. This is it.

God isn't calling the version of you with polished answers and a perfect résumé. He's calling the real, raw, available you.

Someone's healing is waiting. And your yes might be the very thing that unlocks the next chapter of someone else's story.

We don't need to overcomplicate the Great Commission; we don't need to launch a movement. We just need to engage in simple, sustainable, and intentional relationships.

Let's stop hiding. Let's stop spectating. Let's start seeking.

Let's go find them.

Let's be found.

Let's stop playing hide-and-seek … and start connecting with the people God has placed around us.

· ·

Reflection and Intention
Chapter Summary: Don't Discount Yourself

- God has always *called the unlikely*—Moses with a stutter, Mary with no résumé, fishermen with no seminary degrees. What qualified them was not their skill but their surrender.

- The church often paralyzes ordinary believers by *outsourcing evangelism to professionals*. But Scripture is clear: *The Great Commission is not reserved for the few* but *entrusted to the many*.

- *Your voice matters*. People are assigned to it. Saul did not need Peter—he needed Ananias. Someone's breakthrough may be waiting on your obedience.

- Evangelism is not about conversion quotas, titles, or stages. It is about *blessing*, listening, serving, and carrying the healing presence of Jesus into everyday life.
- You don't need a title to disciple. You don't need permission to love. You don't need credentials to say yes. *God isn't waiting for your polish—he's waiting for your surrender.*

Reflection Questions: A Personal Assessment

Sit with these for a few minutes and let the Spirit search your heart.

- When you think of evangelism, do you instinctively assume it belongs to pastors, missionaries, or "special" Christians? Why?
- In what ways have you discounted yourself—believing you're too ordinary, too broken, or too unqualified to disciple others?
- Who has been "Ananias" in your life—an ordinary person God used to awaken your faith?
- Whom might God be asking you to be "Ananias" for right now? What's stopping you from stepping into that role?
- If evangelism is blessing, not selling, what is one simple act of blessing you can extend this week?

Breath Prayer

As you move forward, pause to say this simple breath prayer throughout your day:

Inhale: *Lord, You can use me.*
Exhale: *I say yes.*

part two

CARRY THE MISSION

5

be a story catcher

Listening is much more than allowing another to talk while waiting for a chance to respond. Listening is paying full attention to others and welcoming them into our very being.

Henri J. M. Nouwen

WE ARE LIVING in days when headlines scream louder than hope. The world is groaning with unrest—wars and rumors of wars, rising hatred, political division, cultural confusion, and spiritual apathy. People aren't just scrolling through chaos—they're *living* in it. And here's what's tragic: In the noise of it all, no one feels heard.

But what if God is calling us not just to preach louder but to listen deeper?

Everyone has a story. And everyone wants someone to hear it. But here's the question—are we really listening?

We were created in the image of a God who *speaks*—but also a God who *listens*. Yet most people today feel invisible, overlooked, unheard. Social media has made us more connected but more lonely than ever. We're flooded with opinions but starved for empathy.

> *The church cannot afford to be tone-deaf. We can't afford to be more interested in* making statements *than* making space. *Because if the church isn't listening, then who is?*

In times like these, the church cannot afford to be tone-deaf. We can't afford to be more interested in *making statements* than *making space*. Because if the church isn't listening, then who is?

See, in most conversations about evangelism, we're trained to be story*tellers*. We prep our three-minute testimony, memorize key verses, and learn to "close the deal." But in evangelship—where evangelism and discipleship intertwine like roots and fruit—the first move isn't to speak. The first move is to *catch the story*.

Yeah, I said it. Before you tell someone about your story or God's story, you've got to be willing to catch *theirs*.

Eugene Peterson, in his book *The Contemplative Pastor*, states that "The work of listening is so much more demanding than talking: listening requires unselfishness and humility."[1] Hence, catching stories isn't passive; it's active spiritual work that requires humility—a humility that urges the hearer to make it more about others, and less about themselves.

People will tell you who they are if you listen long enough. They'll tell you what they value, what hurts them, what they dream about at night. But only if you're paying attention. Only if you stick around.

> *If we're not willing to be story catchers, we'll never be trusted as truth carriers.*

If we're not willing to be story catchers, we'll never be trusted as truth carriers.

Why? Because when people feel heard, they feel seen. And

when they feel seen, they open their hearts. As theologian and counselor David Augsburger once wrote, "Being heard is so close to being loved that for the average person, they are almost indistinguishable."[2] Listening isn't just polite; it's prophetic. It tells the other person, "you matter."

This isn't soft spirituality—it's spiritual warfare. In today's culture, the enemy is stealing identity, purpose, and hope from many people. Our weapon is presence. Our posture is listening. Our power is found in empathy paired with truth.

Let me be prophetic with you for a second. There is a window of time we've been given. A moment in history where hearts are tender, even if people act tough. Where culture is shaking, and people are searching. Where identity is being redefined, and people are desperate for something real.

This is not the time to play it safe. This is not the time to retreat. This is the time to step up. Luke 10:2 says, "The harvest is plentiful, but the workers are few. Ask the Lord of the harvest, therefore, to send out workers into his harvest field."

Workers don't just preach. They listen. They discern. They enter stories, not platforms.

Let me tell you mine.

My Story

I grew up in a broken home. My dad walked out on my mom the *night* of their wedding. So yeah—I never had a dad growing up. And in my neighborhood, where all the other kids had theirs around, I felt that absence *loudly*.

One day, I asked my *abuela*, "Where's my dad?" She paused, looked up at a painting on the wall, pointed to it, and said in Spanish, *"Ese es tu papa … Papá Dios."* Father God.

I didn't question it. I *believed* her.

So much so that one day, I went to a friend's house and saw the same painting on his wall. I got excited. I pointed and asked him, "You know my dad, too?"

He looked at me like I had three heads and said, "Dude, that's Jesus … you dork!"

Now, you may laugh, but I'm telling you—that was real for me. My grandma told me about Jesus like he was family. I loved hearing stories about him—how he healed people, how he calmed storms, how he was always near. And in my heart, he became *my Father*.

Fast-forward a few years: I'm sitting in a Baptist church for the first time, and the preacher is going in. I turn to my aunt, who brought me to the church, and ask her, "Who's he talking about?"

She says, "*Papá Dios* … the same one grandma has on the wall."

Then she asks me, "Do you want him in your heart?"

Without hesitation, I say, "Yes."

Now, I didn't fully surrender to Jesus right then, but my heart opened up that day. I became curious. Receptive. My aunt bought me my first Bible to read, and I loved it! The stories stuck with me, and little moments throughout my life kept reminding me—*he's real, and he's near.*

Even in geometry class. Yep. Geometry.

Now, listen, I hated geometry. Still do. My test scores back me up. But one day, I actually studied. I took the test, grinding through each question until I hit the dreaded bonus question: number 20. I had no clue.

And then, something miraculous (or mischievous) happened. The girl in front of me—let's just say she was the class Einstein—had long hair that usually blocked my view. But that day, she flipped it to the other side, and *boom*—I saw the answer clear as day. I swear I heard angels sing. Heaven opened up.

So I wrote my answer down. (Wink, wink.)

A week later, Mr. Lee, my geometry teacher, passed back our tests. I couldn't believe it—100 percent. What I didn't know was that only two people in the class got perfect scores … me and the hair-flipping Einstein.

Mr. Lee started calling students to solve problems on the board. He was calling everyone *but* me. I was thinking I got away with it! But then he said, "Larry, why don't you do number 20?"

Yo … I died inside.

I took the slowest walk of my life to that board. Sweat pouring, I was praying for the bell to ring. Maybe the building could catch fire. Anything.

Everyone else finished their problems while I stood there, frozen. Then Mr. Lee said something I'll never forget:

"Larry … are you ready?"

I turned around and confessed, "Sir, I guessed on number 20."

He looked at the class and said, "This, class, is what it looks like when you cheat."

Ouch.

But then he pulled me aside after class. And what he said next changed my life.

"Mr. Perez," he said, "this moment doesn't have to define you." He took time to know my story that day. He asked me about my family background, already knowing I came from a broken home and that I wasn't into gangs but was an athlete. He then went on to tell me, "I'm going to give you an opportunity to make it right."

I was confused. "How?"

He said, "There's a church that meets in a school nearby. I want you to go for the next two months. Come back each Monday and give me a report on what you learned."

So I did as he said. Every week we met, he knew more about

me, and I knew more about what I was observing and hearing at the church.

What I didn't realize then was that Mr. Lee was discipling me. In his own way, he caught my story and was doing evangelship.

Grandma taught me how to *believe* in God.

Aunty "Nani" gave me my first Bible, helping me *know* more about God.

Mr. Lee taught me how to *walk* with God.

Looking back, I see how God used each person in my story. Not with a bullhorn. Not with a stage. But with open ears and intentional steps. They caught my story—and used it to help me see God's story more clearly.

That's why evangelship demands a different approach. We don't just rush in to speak. We *stay* to listen. Because once you catch someone's story, you earn the right to share your own.

Mr. Lee could have let our cultural differences keep him distant—I am Latino and he is Korean. Instead, he was willing to cross cultural boundaries because he knew that the gospel was never meant to stay in one place, and that to catch a story we have to be willing to catch even those whose lives are different from ours.

So the next time you're with someone at work, school, the gym, or even on a random bus ride, don't be so quick to *preach*. Ask a question. Listen deeply. Stay long enough to catch the story.

Because every story caught is an opportunity for the gospel to be felt—not just heard.

The Gospel Was Never Meant to Stay in One Place

Catching someone's story, then, isn't just about empathy—it's about mission. When we lean in long enough to really hear, we discover that the gospel is already pressing against the edges of culture, longing to break through walls of language, background, and experience. My own story only makes sense because others were willing to step across those boundaries to meet me where I was.

Evangelship doesn't stay confined to what's comfortable. It compels us outward because the gospel was never meant to stay in one place. If every story matters, then every boundary is worth crossing. From the very beginning, the gospel was crossing lines—cultural, economic, political, and personal. It was never meant to stay safely tucked inside one language, one nation, or one social class. One of the reasons the good news is good is that it's for *everyone*. That's the vision God gives us in Revelation 7:9: "A great multitude that no one could count, from every nation, tribe, people and language."

But if we take a hard look at our churches, small groups, and dinner tables, we often see the opposite. We gather with people who look like us, think like us, vote like us. Not necessarily because we're trying to be exclusive, but because it's easier. Familiarity feels safe. Comfort feels right.

But Jesus didn't come to make us comfortable. He came to make us faithful.

> *Jesus didn't come to make us comfortable. He came to make us faithful.*

Catching stories across boundaries isn't always easy. It calls us to live differently. It calls us to *go*, not just invite. To cross boundaries, not build fences. To listen before we speak. To meet people in their culture, in their story, and point to where God is already at work.

One of the most radical aspects of Jesus' ministry was his refusal to stick to one crowd. He healed a Roman centurion's servant. He crossed deep cultural divides to talk with a Samaritan woman at a well. He invited himself over to Zacchaeus's house—a tax collector and therefore a traitor in many eyes.

In each case, Jesus stepped outside what was comfortable or expected. He didn't flatten people into categories or shy away from the mess of their lives. He engaged. He listened. He spoke truth *through* relationship, not around it.

And here's the lesson: If we want to reach people who've been overlooked or disillusioned by religion, we need to stop assuming we already know what they need. We need to sit down, hear their story, and look for where God is already writing something beautiful—even if it doesn't look like it yet. This principle of holistic, attentive engagement was beautifully modeled by one of the church's key early writers.

The Doctor's Prescription

Allow me to take a minute and talk to you about someone who doesn't always get the spotlight but played a huge part in shaping what we know about Jesus and the early church and the importance of evangelship.

I'm talking about Luke. Yep, that Luke—the doctor. A Gentile. A man who didn't grow up in church, didn't memorize Torah verses as a kid, probably came from a home that wasn't checking in with Yahweh on the daily. Maybe his family worshipped other gods. Maybe they just weren't religious at all. But one thing's for sure: Luke wasn't a native to this faith. He was a convert. And what he did with it? Man, it's inspiring.

Luke met Paul in the city of Troas (see Acts 16). Paul was dealing with some kind of physical issue. We're not totally sure what it was, but it's likely what led him to Luke in the first place. From that moment on, Luke didn't just record Paul's journey—he joined it. The narrative in Acts shifts from "they" to "we" (Acts 16:10), signaling that Luke is now part of the story himself. From that point forward, they did life together—ministry, travel, suffering, and victory—all of it.[3]

Now, Luke wasn't one of the twelve disciples. But make no mistake—he was a disciple. A follower of Jesus. Out of all the Gospel writers, Luke gives us the most detailed account of Jesus' life, especially his birth. Why? Because Luke was a researcher, a storyteller, a man of detail, a man on a mission. And he didn't stop there—he also wrote the book of Acts.

Between the twenty-four chapters in the Gospel of Luke and the twenty-eight in Acts, Luke gives us the longest contribution to the New Testament. And here's what gets me: He didn't grow up in this. He *chose* it. He received the faith and then passed it on. That matters.

Let's look at the start of the book of Luke:

> Many have undertaken to draw up an account of the things that have been fulfilled among us, just as they were handed down to us by those who from the first were eyewitnesses and servants of the word. With this in mind, since I myself have carefully investigated everything from the beginning, I too decided to write an orderly account for you, most excellent Theophilus, so that you may know the certainty of the things you have been taught.
>
> LUKE 1:1–4

From this passage, we can see three key ways Luke approached evangelship.

He was methodical. Luke says, "I too decided to write an *orderly* account." That word "orderly" matters; he wanted his reader to be sure. To have confidence. Certainty. Why? Because the man he's writing to, Theophilus, was struggling with uncertainty. Sound familiar? The vast majority of people today, especially in America, have *heard* of Jesus. They know the Christmas story. They know about the cross. But they're not *certain*. They're not *convinced*. They're walking around with a vague belief but no anchored faith. Luke's writing is for them.

He was relational. Now, who exactly is Theophilus? Some folks think he might be a made-up person, like a symbolic title for "lover of God." But I don't think so. I believe he was a real person, and because Luke calls him "Most Excellent Theophilus," which was a term used in Roman culture to address officials, it's likely that Theophilus was a Roman official of some kind. Maybe Luke was his doctor. Maybe they had some sort of personal connection. But either way, Luke cared enough to write this *massive* letter—*over sixty pages long!*—to help Theophilus move from uncertainty to truth. That's love. That's mission. That's intentionality. Luke didn't just throw Theophilus a tract; he poured months of labor into a personal, trustworthy, and lengthy explanation.

He was personal. Luke didn't just copy and paste what was already out there. He didn't hand off the Gospel of Matthew or the Gospel of John. He wrote his own account. Why? Because he had a unique voice. A different angle. The Gospels were written with different audiences in mind. Matthew's is aimed at the Jewish crowd. John's is more poetic and theological. But Luke? Luke is writing to someone like himself—a Gentile. Someone who wasn't raised in the Jewish faith, but is curious, searching, hungry.

Story catching isn't just about hearing someone's story—it's about letting their questions shape how we share truth.

Luke shows us that story catching isn't just about hearing someone's story—it's about letting their questions shape how we share truth. To really reach people, we've got to know them. Catch their story. Acknowledge their doubts.

And then, once we become a story catcher, it leads us to understand how to become good storytellers by sharing the truth of Jesus in a way that connects. That lands. That clicks. That's not a five-minute project. Sometimes it's five hours. Or five years. But do we love people enough to walk that long road with them? Clearly, Luke did. Because he didn't stop with one book.

When you flip over to Acts, you see something subtle but important. In Luke 1:3, he says, "most excellent Theophilus." But in Acts 1:1? He just says, "Theophilus." No title. No formality.

Why? Something's changed.

Maybe Theophilus is no longer in public office; maybe he stepped down. But I think it's deeper than that. I think he became a brother in Christ. And when you're in the family, you don't call each other "most excellent." That'd be weird. (Though, hey, if you *really* want to, you can call me that—just kidding!)

The Gospel of Luke is all about what Jesus *began* to do and teach. But Acts? Acts is about what Jesus is *continuing* to do and teach—through the church, through his disciples. Luke's first book is evangelism. His second book is discipleship. You can't have one without the other. That's the rhythm. The pattern. First, we come to know Jesus—then we learn to walk with him, grow in him, and go out empowered by the Spirit to expand his kingdom.

And that's where we, as the church, come in.

Because what Luke wrote to Theophilus back then? It's still relevant today. His orderly account—his deep research, his heart, his boldness—all points us toward a simple but profound mission: Love people

Love people enough to meet them where they are ... and walk with them until they find certainty.

enough to meet them where they are ... and walk with them until they find certainty.

So, the question for us isn't just *what* do we know—it's who is our Theophilus? Who are we writing to? Who are we investing in? Who are we willing to walk with—however long it takes—so they can move from confusion to clarity, from doubt to discipleship?

The hard truth is we can't answer those questions if we remain isolated in familiar spaces.

Breaking the Bubble

For many Christians, their social circles are an echo chamber. They interact with people who share their worldview, reinforcing the same perspectives and cultural assumptions. But Jesus calls his followers to more. Evangelship requires us to be intentional about breaking the bubble. This isn't just about stepping into unfamiliar spaces—it's about catching the stories that emerge in those spaces. When we take time to hear someone's story, we honor their humanity and create space for the gospel to take root. Here are three practical ways to begin:

Evaluate your current circle. Who are the people you interact with daily? Are they diverse in thought, background, and experience? Or do they mostly reflect your own identity?

Step into unfamiliar spaces. Attend community events, volunteer with organizations that serve different populations, or simply strike up conversations with coworkers and neighbors who have different perspectives.

Listen before you speak. People are more open to the gospel when they feel heard. Ask genuine questions about their culture, experiences, and beliefs without rushing to correct or debate.

All these things require intentionality, humility, and a deep willingness to enter another person's world. This radical mindset—this willingness to become all things to all people—is the approach Paul advocated in 1 Corinthians 9:22: "I have become all things to all people so that by all possible means I might save some."

This does not mean compromising truth but rather building bridges so the truth can be received.

Paul's ability to build those bridges goes much deeper than just reaching out. Earlier in this passage, he states, "Though I am free and belong to no one, I have made myself a slave to everyone, to win as many as possible" (v.19).

Paul could become "all things to all people" because he was first "free from all." His freedom was rooted in a secure identity in Christ. This allowed him to enter uncomfortable realities with love, not fear. He was not seeking validation, nor manipulating others— he was free to serve. This freedom is profound for evangelship, as we can only truly love others when we are free from needing them. If we find it challenging to approach those outside our circles, is it possible that we have yet to find the true freedom Paul describes? We need a deep understanding of this gospel freedom so that we can cross over and become bridges for others as we catch their stories.

Learning to Cross Cultures

This kind of work starts with cultural intelligence (CQ), which is basically the ability to function well in a variety of cultural settings. It includes:

- **Curiosity:** Do I want to understand other cultures?
- **Knowledge:** Do I understand the differences?
- **Strategy:** Can I prepare for cross-cultural interactions?
- **Action:** Am I willing to adapt when the moment comes?

And here's the key: This isn't just for missionaries or pastors. This is for all of us. Anyone who wants to reach beyond their usual bubble—to be a neighbor, a friend, a disciple-maker in a multicultural world—needs these tools.

When you go to work, to the barber shop, to the grocery store—you're already walking through diverse spaces. The question is whether you're truly seeing the people there. Do you know their stories? Their history? Their pain? Their joy?

For example, the Latino community in the US isn't a monolith. It includes people from over twenty countries, each with unique traditions, languages, and beliefs. Even the Spanish language changes from region to region. What might be a friendly phrase in one culture could be offensive in another. Understanding these nuances matters.

Latinos also carry a rich, complex spiritual heritage—one shaped by colonization, migration, oppression, family, and resilience. Some may have inherited faith traditions. Others may have been turned off by religion entirely. But all of them carry stories that matter, and those stories shape how they hear the gospel.

If we want to engage with people meaningfully, we need to listen first. We need to ask questions. We need to examine our assumptions, and sometimes, unlearn them. That commitment to see and hear people's stories, not their categories, is what it means to walk through Samaria instead of around it.

Catching the Story, Finding God at Work

Let me tell you what this looks like in real life.

A couple from my church came to me once and asked if I'd consider officiating their niece's wedding. She was a Christian, and her nonnegotiable was getting married in a church. Her fiancé came from a Buddhist family—but said he was open to it.

Every pastor they'd approached before had turned them down. I didn't give an answer right away. I said, "I'd be willing to *talk* with them. No promises, but I'll listen."

As it turned out, I already had a trip planned to Tampa for seminary. Coincidentally—or not—that's where they lived. We scheduled a meeting, but the couple had a scheduling conflict. Only the groom-to-be could meet. So we grabbed dinner at Applebee's.

I asked him to tell me his story.

What he shared wrecked me.

He'd been a nightclub bouncer. One night, he got into a violent fight while trying to protect someone and ended up in jail. While there, he met a cellmate who introduced him to the Bible. For a moment, the gospel began to take root. But eventually that same cellmate revealed himself to be a hypocrite—talking about Jesus but not living like him. The young man walked away disillusioned.

After his release, he was riding his motorcycle and hit a pothole. Launched into the air, he somehow landed on his feet—completely unharmed. Shaken, he walked into the nearest restaurant to catch his breath. And that's where he met the woman who would become his fiancée.

I just sat back and said, "Man, God is *all over* your story."

He looked confused. So I walked him through it: God planting seeds in jail. God sparing his life in that crash. God leading him to a restaurant where the waitress just happened to be the woman who would introduce him to faith again. I said, "You think this journey is just about marrying her ... but maybe God's been chasing you down this whole time. Because I believe God wants to marry you!"

Right there in the middle of Applebee's, tears started rolling down his face.

He didn't say yes to Jesus that night—but the wall cracked. We kept meeting. We talked about his doubts. He asked hard questions. And eventually, I had the honor of officiating their wedding. They're attending church together now. They're building something rooted and real.

I didn't bend my convictions. I didn't dilute the gospel. But I did choose to *sit down and listen.*

Be a story catcher before you become a storyteller. Because if you listen long enough, you'll hear where God is already moving.

That's the heartbeat of evangelship: Be a story catcher before you become a storyteller. Because if you listen long enough, you'll hear where God is already moving.

The Courage to Go

It's okay if your church started out mostly monocultural. That's often how communities form. But that doesn't have to be where the story ends.

Jesus didn't stay where it was comfortable, and neither should we. He didn't say, "Go into all the nations—unless it's awkward." He said, "Go." Period.

We live in neighborhoods and cities filled with cultural richness. You can't reach people meaningfully without learning what shaped them. You can't love someone well if you're not willing to understand where they come from. This takes cultural humility. It takes curiosity. It takes story catching. It takes asking, "Who's in my circle? Who's not? And what am I willing to do about it?"

It also takes courage to shift the way we do ministry—not just inviting people to our table but sometimes getting up and going to *theirs.* Because this is where the kingdom gets real. When we stop organizing our lives around comfort and start organizing them around Jesus' call to *go, listen,* and *disciple,* we become part of a bigger story—one that includes every nation, every tribe, every tongue. And maybe—just maybe—every Applebee's, too.

. . . .

Reflection and Intention
Chapter Summary: Becoming a Story Catcher

- Evangelship begins not with speaking but with *listening*. In a world where headlines scream louder than hope, and loneliness grows deeper than connection, *people long to be heard*. To catch a story is to *honor a person's dignity* and *open a door for the gospel* to be received.

- From Luke's careful research for Theophilus to Jesus' willingness to cross cultural boundaries, we see that *listening is not passive*—it's evangelship in motion. It's how we *discern* where God is already at work and join him there.

- Story catching requires *humility, curiosity,* and *courage*. It means *breaking out of our echo chambers,* crossing cultures, and stepping into unfamiliar spaces to hear stories different from our own.

- When people feel heard, they feel *seen*. And when they feel seen, their *hearts open to the One* who has been pursuing them all along.

- Evangelship is not just telling the truth—it's *embodying the truth* with presence, patience, and love. *Listening is the first act of mission.*

Reflection Questions: A Personal Assessment
Take a few quiet moments to reflect on these questions. Write honestly. Let God stretch you as you consider your answers.

- Who in your life right now needs you to slow down and truly listen?
- Do you tend to rush into speaking, teaching, or correcting before you've caught someone's story? Why do you think that is?
- What boundaries—cultural, social, or personal—do you find hardest to cross when it comes to listening to others?
- Think about your everyday circles (work, school, neighborhood, church). Whose voices are missing? Whose stories have you not taken time to hear?

Breath Prayer

Use this prayer to center yourself as you practice story catching:

Inhale: *Lord, open my ears to hear.*
Exhale: *Lord, open my heart to love.*

6

go where the people are

Radically ordinary hospitality is this: using your Christian home in a daily way that seeks to make strangers neighbors, and neighbors family of God.

Rosaria Butterfield

PICTURE FLORIDA: SUNSHINE blazing, kids cannonballing into a neighborhood pool, the air filled with laughter and chlorine. Smack in the middle of 275 homes, that patch of concrete and water was nothing special. Yet somehow, it became holy ground.

Two friends, Judy and Samantha, lived in that neighborhood. They shared a Bible study, a deep desire to be present where God had placed them, and eight kids between their two families. They didn't set out to start a ministry. They were just doing life—chatting by the pool, loving their kids, and showing up consistently. When conversations turned deeper, they'd say, "We meet on Tuesdays. Want to come?"

Simple. No pressure. Just real relationships building real bridges.

And then came Joyce.

She had just moved from Chicago, where she thrived as a full-time architect. Now? She was learning the slow chaos of stay-at-home motherhood: nap schedules, tantrums, and potty-training. She was lonely. Overwhelmed. And then she met Judy and Samantha.

From day one, they welcomed her in. No sermon. No sales pitch. Just kindness.

Joyce watched the eight kids play while two moms somehow didn't lose their minds. She asked, "How do you get your kids to nap?" "How did you survive potty training?" They answered with laughter and honesty—sacred conversations disguised as everyday small talk.

Eventually, they offered the same invitation: "Tuesday Bible study. Want to come?"

Joyce didn't flinch. "I'm an atheist," she said plainly.

Judy just smiled. "We have childcare."

Joyce blinked. "Okay, I'll come."

That's where the crack in the wall began—not because she was seeking God, but because she needed a break.

Except she didn't leave. She stayed with her son that first day, arms crossed, heart closed. "I don't believe any of this," she said.

But she kept coming. Week after week. Because her son loved it.

Little by little, something shifted. Her posture softened. Her curiosity stirred. She picked up a study guide. Then a Bible. Then a commentary. One day, she walked in with a tote bag full of notes and questions—no longer the skeptic in the back but the most engaged voice in the room.

She never got baptized. Never made a declaration of faith. But she brought her neighbor Lynn, another woman with no religious background. And Lynn? She met Jesus. Her whole family was baptized.

And here's the truth that should stop us in our tracks: Joyce never said yes to Jesus—but she made space. And that space paved the way for someone else's salvation.

The pool wasn't a pulpit. But it became a sanctuary.

Jesus' Ministry Beyond the Temple

One of the most striking aspects of Jesus' earthly ministry was where he chose to do his work, and who he chose to do his work with.

While he occasionally taught in synagogues, his most impactful moments happened outside religious institutions—on hillsides, at dinner tables, in fishing boats, and on dusty roads. He met people in their everyday lives, stepping into their brokenness rather than waiting for them to come to him.

In Mark 2:17, Jesus states: "It is not the healthy who need a doctor, but the sick. I have not come to call the righteous, but sinners."

Jesus understood that the lost, hurting, and broken were not always sitting in the pews of the synagogue; they were out in the streets, in their homes, and in their workplaces. He pursued them, making himself present in their reality. If the church today wants to see revival, it must reclaim this method—going to where people are rather than expecting them to come to us.

If the church today wants to see revival, it must reclaim this method—going to where people are rather than expecting them to come to us.

Consider the woman with the issue of blood (Luke 8:43–48).

She didn't meet Jesus in a temple; she encountered him on the street. Zacchaeus, the tax collector (Luke 19:1–10), didn't have a life-changing moment in a synagogue; Jesus called him down from a tree and went to his house for dinner. Time and again, Jesus sought out those whom society overlooked.

Jesus didn't just teach in synagogues or lecture from a scroll. He also taught as he walked. As he sat at a table. As he entered a new town. His classroom was the street, the shoreline, the dinner party, the interruption. His method was life-on-life—and it was deeply relational. He didn't just make converts. He made disciples. People who learned not just *what* he said, but *how* he lived.

And he didn't stop there. He trained his followers not to make disciples for *themselves*—but for *him*. He warned them not to seek status or titles, saying, "Don't aim to be called teacher or master. Just follow me—and help others do the same" (Matthew 23:8–10, my paraphrase).

Jesus wasn't interested in building fan clubs. He was building a movement of people who would humbly invite others into the same journey they were on.

That's the difference between spiritual leadership and spiritual ego. Jesus wasn't interested in building fan clubs. He was building a movement of people who would humbly invite others into the same journey they were on.

And here's what's wild: Jesus didn't even wait for people to apply. He initiated the call. He went first. He looked at Peter, Andrew, James, John—working their fishing nets—and simply said, "Follow me." He walked past a tax collector's booth and said, "You too." That kind of personal invitation was uncommon, because of who he called. It's exactly how Jesus works. He still does.

So if you're wondering how to engage people in your neighborhood, your workplace, your grocery store—take a cue from Jesus: Don't wait for them to come to you. Go to them. Listen to their stories. Start with a conversation. An invitation. A simple act of kindness. You don't need a stage or a platform or a degree. You just need to be willing to go where people already are—and invite them into your life.

Jesus didn't disciple from a distance. He walked with people. And as his followers, that's our call, too.

The Difference Between Drawing Lines and Building Direction

This commitment to walking with people requires a fundamental shift in mindset. If we continue to operate like a club waiting for members to show up, we'll miss the movement and fail to reach the harvest.

The Western church has largely adopted a "come and see" model of evangelism. In this model, church buildings function as destinations, and outreach efforts often revolve around inviting people into the sanctuary.

When we talk about how we approach belonging and spiritual transformation, we must be honest: Too many churches still approach this by drawing lines. This approach, where the community is defined by a rigid perimeter, is what missiologist Paul Hiebert described as *bounded-set thinking*.[1]

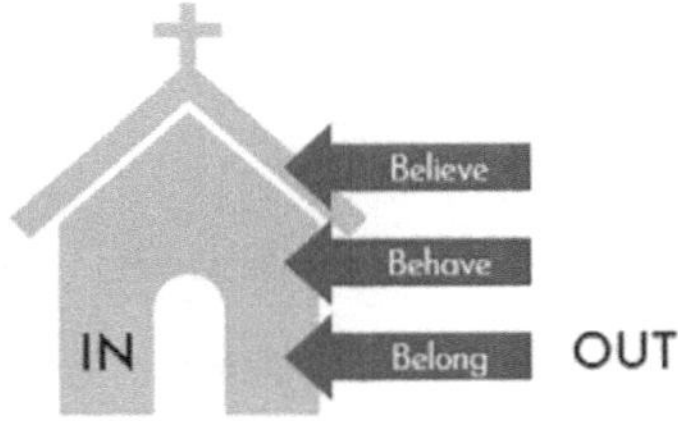

In a bounded-set model, the most important question is whether someone is "in" or "out." A person belongs only if their beliefs and behaviors match the group's established rules. Churches operating this way often focus on getting people to cross a clear boundary—a hand raised during an altar call, a prayer recited, or a name written on a membership roll. Once you've crossed the line, you're in. Whether or not your life actually changes or your relationship with God deepens is secondary. This kind of thinking can unintentionally treat faith like a onetime transaction. It says: *As long as you checked the box, you're good.* But what if someone never comes back? What if they're not growing? What if they never felt connected to begin with? A rigid focus on boundary and membership leaves no room for the messiness of growth.

Jesus modeled a *centered-set* perspective that prioritized relationship and trajectory over boundary and transaction. That's where centered-set thinking offers a much more helpful lens— especially if we want to meet people where they are.

In a centered-set model, the focus isn't on drawing a boundary. Instead, it's on direction. People aren't divided into "in" or "out." They're seen as either moving toward Jesus or away from him.

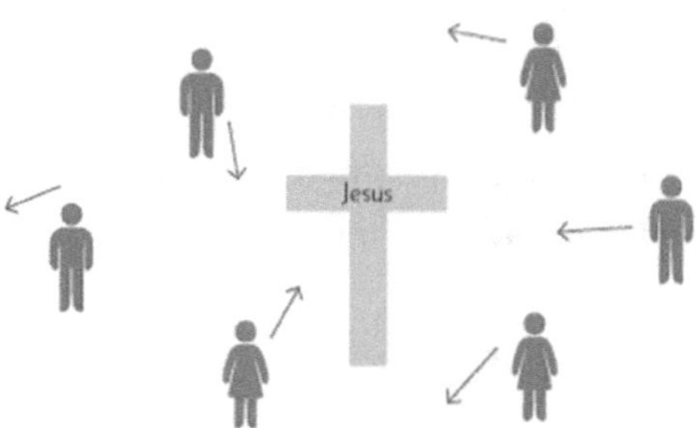

The question isn't whether someone has arrived; it's whether they're headed toward the center. That center—Christ—is the focus, and everyone is invited to keep journeying closer.

In this view, it doesn't matter how far someone starts from the center. What matters is the direction they're pointed. Someone with just a spark of curiosity, asking spiritual questions for the first time, is just as valued as someone who's been faithfully walking with Christ for years. Everyone is somewhere on the path—and everyone is welcome to take the next step.

This mindset fundamentally shifts how we approach evangelship. Because the focus is now on the direction of the heart, the old "come and see" mindset is no longer viable. Our acceptance of where people are on their journey must compel us to "go and tell."

Faith becomes less about passing a test or joining a club and more about a lived, relational process. As one writer puts it, conversion isn't just a moment—it's a metamorphosis. It's not a rupture; it's a transformation over time.[2]

And that's good news, because transformation doesn't happen in isolation. It happens in relationship—when we choose to step into people's lives and journeys, right where they are, rather than demand they join our club before we start discipling them. So instead of obsessing over the bounded-set question of whether someone is "in" or "out," maybe it's time we start asking better questions: *Are they moving toward the center? And how can we walk with them on the way?*

Yet many modern churches function in ways that make it difficult for the lost to engage. Programs, services, and small groups cater primarily to those already inside. While these ministries are valuable, they often fail to meet people in the rawness of their daily struggles.

Evangelship rejects the idea that discipleship happens only within church walls, for those who are already "in." Instead, it encourages believers to actively go into their communities, workplaces, and social spaces to build relationships and disciple people toward Jesus, wherever they currently are.

Breaking the Barriers

For evangelship to take root, the church must break free from the mentality that ministry happens only within designated sacred spaces. Jesus didn't wait for the world to come to him—he went to the world. Evangelship doesn't force people into religious spaces; it brings Jesus into theirs.

> *Evangelship doesn't force people into religious spaces; it brings Jesus into theirs.*

A few years ago, I started frequenting a local coffee shop. I wasn't there to preach; I was just there, present, getting to know the baristas and the regulars. Over time, conversations about life turned into conversations about faith. One barista, Jen, had been burned by church experiences in her youth. She had no intention of ever going back. But because I met her in her space, on her terms, she felt safe asking questions. Months later, she showed up at a Bible study—not because I invited her to church but because she encountered Jesus through simple, daily interactions.

If believers today are to follow Jesus' model, they must step out of their comfort zones and engage with people in their daily realities.

So, what does this look like in practice? It means having intentional conversations with coworkers instead of just inviting them to church. It means engaging in community events, supporting local businesses, and being a consistent presence in the places where people naturally gather. It means seeing grocery stores, gyms, and coffee shops as mission fields, not just errands to check off a list.

When Jesus called his disciples, he didn't say, "Stay here and wait for people to find you." He gave them the Great Commission: "*Go* and make disciples of all nations" (Matthew 28:19, emphasis added). The church must take this command seriously. If we want to see transformation, we must go where the people are.

The call to go is driven by Jesus' own vision of a waiting harvest. The centered-set view allows us to see people the way Jesus did—not as outsiders to be judged but as a harvest ready for gathering:

> When he saw the crowds, he had compassion on them, because they were harassed and helpless, like sheep without a shepherd. Then he said to his disciples, "The harvest is plentiful, but the workers are few. Ask the Lord of the harvest, therefore, to send out workers into his harvest field."
>
> MATTHEW 9:36–38

The harvest isn't defined by who's "in" or who's "out"; it's defined by who's moving toward the center. Evangelship equips believers to step into people's lives, moving beyond passive faith into active engagement with their journey toward Christ. And one way we can be actively engaged is to be people of compassion, following Jesus' example of truly seeing people and meeting their tangible needs.

Meet Needs First

As Christians, we often overcomplicate evangelism. We turn it into programs and pressure. But maybe real evangelship breathes in discipleship and breathes out relationship. Maybe it sounds like "We have childcare" before it sounds like "We have Jesus."

Maybe real evangelship breathes in discipleship and breathes out relationship. Maybe it sounds like "We have childcare" before it sounds like "We have Jesus."

Because Jesus never rushed people into belief. He walked. Sat. Ate. Listened. Invited.

Evangelism isn't about convincing people to believe in Jesus—it's about showing them who he is. And if you look at how Jesus lived, he didn't just preach; he met people's needs.

He healed the sick. He fed the hungry. He welcomed the outcasts. He saw people—really saw them—and met them where they were.

If we want to reach people, we have to do the same.

Before you assume what people need, ask. So often, the church jumps straight into solutions without ever taking the time to understand the problem.

Does your neighbor need prayer, or does she need childcare so she can work?

Does the young man at your church need a Bible, or does he need help paying rent?

Does the single mom need a sermon, or does she need a meal?

People's felt needs aren't always spiritual first. Sometimes, they just need someone to help carry the weight of life. The early church understood this—Acts 2 describes believers selling their possessions and giving to anyone in need. They didn't just talk about Jesus; they lived like him.

Find out what the needs in your community are. Then work with your church, small group, or friends to help meet them.

People don't need to be preached at—they need to be loved. And one of the most powerful ways to love someone is through generosity.

True generosity isn't just giving from excess; it's giving in a way that costs something. It's time, resources, connections, and care. It's opening your home, your wallet, your schedule, and your heart.

It's the difference between saying, "I'll pray for you" and "I'll pray for you now—and here's dinner for your family tonight."

Jesus was radically generous. Not just with his miracles, but with his time, his energy, and ultimately, his life. His generosity wasn't transactional; he didn't give to get. He gave because that's who he was. When we live generously, we reflect him. And that's what changes hearts—not just words but love in action.

It's the first "S" of the B.L.E.S.S. framework we talked about in an earlier chapter—Serve: Meet real needs and love people where they are.

Meeting physical needs doesn't mean ignoring spiritual ones. One of the simplest yet most powerful things you can do is pray—not just *for* people, but *with* them.

> *Prayer isn't a last resort; it's a first response.*

Prayer isn't a last resort; it's a first response.

When someone shares a struggle, don't just say you'll pray later. Stop and pray with them right then and there. It doesn't have to be long or elaborate—just a moment of bringing their need before God.

Because when people see that you genuinely care—not just about their circumstances, but about their soul—that's when they start to wonder what's different about you.

And when they ask, you'll have the answer: Jesus.

The church is at its best when it feels like a family. And in a family, no one goes hungry, no one is forgotten, and no one struggles alone.

We have to stop thinking of generosity as an occasional act and start seeing it as a way of life. A culture of generosity says:

What's mine is yours.
You don't have to do this alone.
I see you, and I care.
Mi casa, su casa.

This is how the church grows—not through bigger buildings or flashier programs, but through simple acts of love that meet real needs.

And when people experience that love, they start to believe in the One who sent it.

. . . .

Reflection and Intention
Chapter Summary: Going Where People Are

- The church must reclaim Jesus' model—going *to the world* rather than waiting for the *world to come to church.*
- Evangelship invites believers to move from a *"come and see"* mindset to a *"go and tell"* lifestyle.
- We must understand the difference between drawing lines and building direction:
  - *Bounded-set* thinking focuses on who's *"in"* or *"out."*
  - *Centered-set* thinking focuses on whether people are *moving toward Jesus.*
- Evangelship is about movement, presence, and intentionality—*taking the love of Jesus into ordinary spaces and relationships.*
- *Radically ordinary hospitality* means using your *home* and *daily life* as a space where *strangers become neighbors,* and *neighbors become family in the faith.*
- *Meeting needs first reflects the heart of Christ;* he healed, fed, and cared for people before teaching them. *Real evangelism starts with compassion and tangible love.*
- *Generosity should be a way of life,* not an occasional act. True generosity costs something—time, energy, and presence.

Reflection Questions: A Personal Assessment

Before moving forward, take a moment to slow down and honestly consider the questions below. They are designed to help you locate where God is already at work in your everyday life.

- Where do you typically expect ministry to happen, and how might Jesus challenge that expectation?
- What does it mean for you to follow Jesus' model of going rather than waiting?
- Do you tend to approach faith by focusing on a boundary line (who's "in" or "out") or by focusing on movement and direction (who's moving toward Jesus)? How does that affect your interactions with non-believers?
- Where has God already placed you—in your work, hobbies, or community—that could be your mission field?
- How often do you use your home or everyday routines as opportunities to love and include others?
- How can you be more intentional about showing up in those spaces with curiosity, compassion, and consistency?

Breath Prayer

When you feel uncertain about your next step, pause and pray:

> **Inhale:** *Draw my heart toward you, Jesus.*
> **Exhale:** *Guide my steps toward those you've called me to serve.*

7

find people of peace

The Person of Peace is the one God has prepared who will open the door to a new community. Our job is not to force the door open, but to find the one God has already prepared.

David Watson

THE CHALLENGE OF evangelship is not simply going but knowing where to focus our limited time and energy. We need to learn how to recognize and invest in the places where the Spirit is already at work.

This is the principle of the person of peace. A person of peace is someone whose heart is open to the gospel, even if they are not yet a believer. They welcome spiritual conversations, extend hospitality, and often influence those around them. Jesus demonstrated this principle in his ministry, seeking out those who were receptive rather than forcing the message on resistant crowds.

Later, we see the early church putting this into practice. The story of Philip and the Ethiopian eunuch in Acts 8 is a perfect example. It's not a story of strategy or stage lights—it's a story of attentiveness to the Spirit's direction. Philip had been part of a big revival in Samaria. The Spirit was clearly at work. But suddenly, God calls him to leave the crowd and head down a wilderness road. No reason. No map. Just go. And Philip goes.

On that road, he meets a man—an Ethiopian official reading the book of Isaiah in his chariot. He's curious, hungry for meaning, but doesn't understand what he's reading. So when Philip asks if he needs help, the man invites him up into the chariot. They sit together. They talk. And through this small, Spirit-led encounter, the gospel moves one step closer to the ends of the earth.

Like the official in the chariot, there are people in your life right now who are already on the edge of an encounter. They simply need a nudge, a guide, and a companion to sit beside them.

What's striking about Philip's story isn't just the encounter itself—it's his readiness. He listens for God's direction. He pays attention to who's around him. And when the moment comes, he doesn't hesitate to step into it.

The eunuch was different from Philip in almost every way—ethnicity, social status, background. Yet Philip recognizes that God is already at work in this man's life and steps into that story, not as a fixer, but as a fellow witness to grace.

God Is Already There

Sometimes we think of evangelism as bringing God into a place. But the truth is, God is already there. He's already moving in the lives of people all around us. The Spirit may be stirring questions in someone's heart long before they ever meet a Christian. Our job is to be ready to join in.

As theologian Isaac Villegas argues in *Migrant God*, "The Bible reminds us that God has been known to join caravans in the wilderness. The Spirit of God dwells with people on the move."[1] So when we talk about being missionaries in our neighborhoods, we're not starting from scratch. We're stepping into stories God is already writing—in workplaces, bus stops, corner stores, classrooms, and yes, even in wilderness roads.

How to Recognize a Person of Peace

This concept is rooted in the instructions Jesus gave to the seventy-two disciples, telling them to look for a "person of peace." Luke 10:5–6 says, "When you enter a house, first say, 'Peace to this house.' If someone who promotes peace is there, your peace will rest on them; if not, it will return to you."

You don't need to be a theologian to live this out. You just need to pay attention. Jesus gave the disciples, and us, clear ways for recognizing where the Spirit has prepared the ground. These are the relational flags that tell us to slow down and invest in these individuals:

> *Jesus gave the disciples, and us, clear ways for recognizing where the Spirit has prepared the ground.*

Welcome: Luke 10:5–6 shows that receptivity is key. When you share the peace of Christ through your attitude, presence, or words, the person of peace is one who accepts it, allowing "your peace [to] rest on them." These people might not look like you. They might not believe like you (yet). But they're open—and that openness is holy ground.

Relationship: In Luke 10:7, Jesus tells the disciples, "Stay there, eating and drinking whatever they give you." The person of peace doesn't only offer a polite greeting; they invite you to stay. Their openness deepens into relationship. They make space for ongoing connection, time around a table, and shared stories, allowing mutual trust to grow. This sustained relational welcome shows that God is cultivating spiritual curiosity and readiness beneath the surface.

Service: A few verses later, Jesus says, "Heal the sick who are there and tell them, 'The kingdom of God has come near to you'" (Luke 10:9). The person of peace allows you to serve them and their community in tangible ways. They're willing to receive prayer, care, or practical help, and often reciprocate that kindness. Their willingness to share needs or invite prayer is a sign of spiritual openness and vulnerability.

Spiritual Curiosity: While not named directly in Luke 10, curiosity flows naturally from the pattern Jesus established. As the disciples stayed and served, the conversation about the kingdom followed. The person of peace becomes curious about your faith, asking questions or seeking understanding. Their interest isn't forced—it grows from relationship and trust, just as it did when the Seventy-Two stayed among the people rather than preaching from a distance.

Influence: Jesus' instructions assume that the peace resting on one household could extend to an entire community. So the person of peace often holds relational influence as they're connected to others who, through them, may also encounter the message of Jesus. Just as Lydia's faith opened doors for her household (Acts 16:15), the person of peace becomes a gateway through whom others experience God's presence.

Jesus' instructions in Luke 10 offer us a practical framework to follow:

- Look for a welcome.
- Stick around and build relationships.

- Serve others with love.
- Watch for curiosity.
- Invest where influence multiplies.

When we find a person of peace, we don't have to manufacture an opportunity for the gospel—it happens naturally. Our role is to cultivate relationships, walk alongside them, and allow the Holy Spirit to work in their hearts. In Western church culture, evangelism is often viewed as a scripted, confrontational approach—knocking on doors, handing out tracts, or making cold invitations to church services. The model of evangelship calls for something different: Rather than pressuring people into a decision, we look for those whom God is already drawing to himself.

Here's the truth: Not everyone will say yes right away. But if someone is *open*—even a little—they're worth leaning into. Jesus said the kingdom of God is like a mustard seed. So don't underestimate what a small crack in the door could become in the hands of a big God.

> *Don't underestimate what a small crack in the door could become in the hands of a big God.*

If they're asking for prayer? That's a seed.

If they're asking how your church is doing? That's a seed.

If they're curious—even skeptical—but willing to listen? That's a seed.

And maybe you're not the one to harvest. Maybe you're just planting. Or watering. Or walking alongside until someone else comes along and finishes the work. Either way, the goal isn't to force it—it's to *join what God is already doing.*

The Rhythm of Discernment

Jesus didn't chase crowds; he invested in those whose hearts were prepared to receive him. If we adopt this same mindset, we will see evangelship become a natural, relational, and life-giving process.

This process requires discernment, which means we don't only focus on surface-level religious actions. Not everyone who goes to the altar is truly ready; they may only be there because of guilt or because their mom wants them to be there. We need to be willing to meet people where they are, recognizing that finding people of peace isn't about forcing doors open—it's about stepping through the ones God has already unlocked.

How do we actively seek out people of peace in our daily lives? It's less about a checklist and more about establishing a spiritual rhythm:

Engage with your community. Be present where people naturally gather—coffee shops, gyms, workplaces, local events.

Pray for open doors. Ask God to guide you toward people whose hearts are ready.

Pay attention to conversations. Who is asking deeper questions? Who seems spiritually curious?

Be patient. Sometimes, spiritual openness takes time. Trust the process and be willing to walk alongside someone in their journey.

When Jesus sent out his disciples, he didn't say, "Convince everyone." He didn't say, "Force it." He said, "Look for those who welcome you."

So many times, we fall into the trap of trying to speak to just anyone without discernment. This approach often leads to high rates of rejection, causing us to become distant, discouraged, and eventually unmotivated because we are constantly pushing against closed doors. We need to be sensitive about being present where God is and joining him in the work. When Jesus sent out his disciples, he didn't say, "Convince everyone." He didn't say, "Force it." He said, "Look for those who welcome you." And if they don't? Dust off your feet and keep moving (Luke 10:10–11). That might sound harsh at first, but it's actually freeing. Jesus knew what many of us still struggle to accept: Some people just aren't ready. And that's okay. Our job isn't to push—it's to *pay attention.*

We need to focus on those who really want change, who God is already working on. That could be that dude who is at your job and is always asking questions about prayer and how church was. Pay attention to the signs.

Not long ago, I had a neighbor who was Muslim. Every time he saw me, he'd ask, "How's church?" He wasn't asking to convert—he was *curious.* He asked questions, not because he wanted a debate, but because something in him wanted to understand.

That's the door. That's the sign.

Then there was a guy at my old job, back when I worked at the probation department. He knew I was a pastor. While others kept it professional, he'd swing by my cubicle and say, "Hey, can you pray for me?" He'd joke around and say, "If I ever walk into a church, it'll catch on fire." But guess what? One day, years later—after I had left the job to go full-time into ministry—he showed up at our church.

I wasn't even there. I was out of the country preaching. But he came looking for me during one of the darkest seasons of his life. Why? Because that seed—the prayers, the little moments— had been planted. And it was our brother Hernandez who did the watering.

Hernandez was serving meals to those in need at the church that day. What makes this even more powerful is that he was serving while battling pancreatic cancer. Hernandez was *dying*, yet still pouring into others. And that testimony broke through to my friend. It wrecked him—in the best way.

Eventually, he gave his life to Jesus. Not because of a single altar call. But because someone prayed, someone served, someone listened. Discipleship happened in the hallway, in the cubicle, at a church during a food outreach.

Later, my friend even led his *own son* to Jesus. That's legacy. That's multiplication. That's evangelship.

A High School Bus Ride and an Unexpected Peace

I'll never forget Tony. He was the kind of kid you didn't want to sit next to on the bus—especially not back in high school. Everyone knew Tony. He was the school bully, the tough guy with gang ties, and the one everyone kept their distance from. But one day, something shifted.

I was just a sophomore, lugging around my football gear, when Tony walked past and gave me a head nod—you know, the kind where you lift your chin as a way to say, "What's up." That little gesture was enough for me to sense an open door. I felt a nudge. So I talked to him.

We got to chatting about football. He mentioned they never let him play. I told him, "That's because they don't know you. If they did, they'd see you could be the scariest player on the team—in a good way." His eyes lit up. "You mean I get to hit people and not get in trouble?" he laughed. That got his attention.

That conversation led to him trying out. And that year, Tony made the team. Not only did he play, but he became a game-changer for us. At the end-of-the-year banquet, our coach—who knew Tony's past—gave him the "Most Improved Player" award.

Tony stood up with tears in his eyes, looked right at me, and said, "Thank you for that bus conversation."

Now, Tony didn't give his life to Jesus that year. But he was *open*. He listened. He responded. He *let someone in*. That's a person of peace. We sometimes expect people of peace to look squeaky clean or sit in the front row of a church, but they might be in the back of the bus with a reputation. All they need is someone to see the crack in the door and walk through it.

> *We sometimes expect people of peace to look squeaky clean or sit in the front row of a church, but they might be in the back of the bus with a reputation.*

Walk Through the Open Doors

A person of peace isn't necessarily the loudest or the most spiritual. They're just *willing to hear*. They might not say yes to Jesus today. But they don't slam the door shut either.

Don't spend your time trying to crack open hearts that aren't ready. Look for the ones who are already cracked open.

Your job isn't to make it grow. That's God's job.

Your job is to notice. To listen. To respond.

To walk through the open doors—and let Jesus do the rest.

. . . .

Reflection and Intention
Chapter Summary: Finding People of Peace

- A *person of peace* is someone God has already prepared—open, curious, and willing to welcome you into their life.

Our task isn't to pry open doors but to notice where the Spirit has already unlocked them.

- Philip and the Ethiopian eunuch show us what this looks like: attentiveness, presence, humility. Philip didn't force his way in—he simply *joined where God was already at work.*
- People of peace can show up in *unexpected places*: on a school bus, in a workplace, in your neighborhood. They may not look like the "ideal candidate," but *their openness is holy ground.*
- *Not everyone is ready, and that's okay.* Evangelship frees us from pressure—our role is to plant seeds, walk through open doors, and let God do the deeper work.

Reflection Questions: A Personal Assessment

As you reflect, allow these questions to tune your heart to the holy invitations hiding in ordinary conversations.

- Who in your life right now shows signs of being a person of peace—welcoming conversation, asking questions, showing openness?
- How have you been tempted to "force the door" in evangelism, rather than discern where God is already at work?
- Think about your own daily rhythms. Are you slowing down enough to notice who's spiritually curious around you?
- Have you ever overlooked someone (like Tony on the bus) because they didn't fit your assumptions of who might be receptive?
- What would it look like for you to shift from "convincing people" to joining God in what he's already stirring?

Breath Prayer

When you sense God might be nudging you toward someone, pause and pray:

> **Inhale:** *Lord, help me notice.*
> **Exhale:** *Open my eyes to your peace already at work.*

8

build friendships of purpose

People who come to know God rarely do so because of one spectacular moment. More often it is through the consistent, faithful witness of ordinary believers living out the gospel daily.

Francis Chan

LET'S BE HONEST—MOST people aren't ready to follow Jesus on day one. And that's okay. It's not always about quick results. But when you show up consistently, when you build real relationships, when people begin to trust you—that's when doors open you never could've imagined.

Let me tell you a story. It's about my son's barber, Micky. He wasn't just any barber—he was probably the one who grew the most out of all the ones I've connected with. At the time, Micky had walked away from God. But every time I sat in that chair, he would really listen when I talked about faith. He'd say, "Man, I love the way you break it down." I could tell the wheels were turning, even if he wasn't all the way there yet.

Eventually, Micky started joining me and my friend Donny on Thursday mornings before the shop opened. We'd take communion together—just three guys hungry for more of God. It was wild to see the spark come back into his eyes, like something was waking up in him.

Micky came from a strong Christian family. He had deep roots. He loved God, but he hadn't stepped into a church building in a long time. Still, over the course of a few years—through steady prayer, time in the Word, and simply doing life together—he found his way back. He reconciled with Jesus, married his fiancée, and now they have a beautiful little girl.

One day, while my son was getting his hair cut, Micky leaned in and said something that really stuck with me. He said, "You know, I remember having my boys in the shop back then, and my oldest, Isaiah—he really got what you were saying."

I had no idea at the time that God was working on more than just Micky.

Fast-forward to Isaiah's junior year of high school. He hit a crossroads—deciding whether he truly believed in Jesus or whether he'd follow the teachings of Islam. But those early seeds? The ones planted while he was just a kid sitting in the shop, quietly listening? They mattered. His dad's testimony, the Word that had soaked into his heart over the years—it helped bridge the gap.

At the beginning of 2025, Isaiah gave his life to Jesus and got baptized. Now he's writing rap music that lifts up Christ. His lyrics are sparking conversations about faith in ways I never could. He's reaching his generation in a language they understand, and his boldness is inspiring others to look at life—and God—differently.

And all of that? It came from just being consistent. From showing up. From building a real relationship instead of rushing a result.

That's the power of faithfulness. That's what happens when we play the long game.

In a world full of grand gestures and short attention spans, what people need most isn't another big event, emotional speech, or viral moment. They need something far more radical—someone who actually sticks around.

> *In a world full of grand gestures and short attention spans, what people need most isn't another big event, emotional speech, or viral moment. They need something far more radical—someone who actually sticks around.*

An Open Door Called Thirst

When Jesus met the Samaritan woman at the well, he didn't begin with a miracle. He didn't launch into a sermon. He didn't shame her for her past or demand that she change.

He asked for a drink. One thirsty person speaking to another.

It's easy to forget that Jesus, fully divine, was also fully human. In that moment, he was tired, hot, and thirsty. And in his vulnerability, he opened the door to a conversation that would change not just one woman's life, but her entire community.

We've been trained to see discipleship as something top-down—teacher to student, expert to beginner, holy to unholy. But evangelship flips that. It says: *I'm broken, too.* It says: *I'm thirsty, too.* It invites people into a shared experience of grace, not a one-way transmission of truth. It's a straight line between two people, both in need of Jesus, walking toward him together.

That's what we're called to do. Not to instruct from a pedestal but to journey with people as friends with purpose. To disciple, not by being above someone but by walking beside them—on the same path, toward the same Savior. Paul said it best in 1 Thessalonians 2:8:

"Because we loved you so much, we were delighted to share with you not only the gospel of God but our lives as well."

> *Evangelship doesn't require a stage, a mic, or a perfect theology. It just requires presence. It requires love. It requires a willingness to get close enough to someone to share not just the message—but your life.*

The truth is, evangelship doesn't require a stage, a mic, or a perfect theology. It just requires presence. It requires love. It requires a willingness to get close enough to someone to share not just the message—but your life.

The Art of Listening

We live in a loud world. Fast-paced, content-driven, full of noise. But the power of listening—really listening—is one of the rarest and most radical ways to nurture a relationship. Earlier, we talked about story catching as a way to open the door to someone's story. But active, ongoing listening is how we continue to be present and attentive, deepening connection and building trust over time.

Jesus was a master at nurturing relationships by demonstrating radical, relational attention. He didn't just listen once and move on; he stayed, he returned, and he walked alongside people through their questions and struggles.

When blind Bartimaeus cried out from the roadside, Jesus didn't assume what the man needed. He asked, "What do you want me to do for you?" (Mark 10:51)—granting him agency and dignity in the conversation. When the woman at the well approached, he didn't start with confrontation. He asked for water. He invited her to speak first, staying long enough to transition the conversation from thirst to living water (John 4). After his resurrection, Jesus found two disciples walking away from Jerusalem, discouraged and confused. He didn't immediately reveal himself. He joined them on the walk to Emmaus, listening to their grief and confusion before gently reteaching them the Scripture over miles, nurturing their broken faith back to life (Luke 24:13–15).

We don't listen to fix people. We listen to *know* them. And when we know them—when we see their humanity, their history, their wounds—we begin to love them not as a project, but as a person. In that sacred space of listening, the Holy Spirit does what only he can do: He makes people feel seen.

Presence over Program

Someone once told me, "Change moves at the speed of trust."

Trust isn't built overnight, and it certainly isn't built by a single conversation or act of kindness. It's built through showing up, time and time again. People are watching for the same thing they saw in Jesus: a friend who will still be there when life gets hard, when the excitement fades, and when the journey to faith takes longer than expected.

Real friends show up even when it's inconvenient. It's easy to show up when it's exciting, when the conversations are deep, or when we feel like we're making a difference. But real friendship is tested in the quiet moments—the ones that feel unremarkable.

Think about the people who have impacted your own life the most. It probably wasn't the person who gave the most inspiring speech, but the one who was there for you. The one who checked in. The one who listened. The one who didn't give up on you, even when you weren't sure you wanted to be helped.

It means:

- Texting to check in, even when they don't text back.
- Showing up to celebrate their wins, even when they don't believe in God yet.

- Walking with them through their struggles, without pushing an agenda.
- Letting your life speak louder than your words.

For a long time, many churches and Christians have approached evangelism like an event—something with a start, a finish, and a box to check. A speaker delivers a message, a crowd listens, and some raise their hands or pray a quick prayer. And while those moments can be powerful and genuine, they can also give the impression that becoming a Christian is mostly about saying yes to a specific invitation rather than entering into a lifelong relationship with Jesus.

If our approach to evangelism focuses mainly on moments, we risk neglecting the slow, relational, transformative process of becoming like Jesus. As Alan Hirsch puts it, "If you use entertainment to win people to faith, then you have to keep entertaining them to keep them on the journey."[1] And eventually, the show stops being enough.

I'm not saying evangelistic events are bad—they can be beautiful starting points. The problem is when we treat them as finish lines. That's why church planter and disciple-maker Ralph Moore reminds us, "Counting the number of people who pray a 90-second prayer means little unless those people mature to reproduce disciples."[2] In other words, the goal is not just converts; it's disciples—people who follow Jesus, day in and day out, and help others do the same.

What if we stopped seeing salvation as just one moment and started viewing it as a journey? That's what some thinkers have tried to express through tools like the Engel Scale—a way to visualize the many small steps someone might take toward faith. From curiosity to understanding, from asking questions to deciding to follow Jesus, each step matters.[3]

Think about your own story. Chances are, it wasn't just one moment. It was a series of nudges. Conversations. Struggles. Aha moments. Relationships. Tears. Healing. God works in all of it—and often long before someone says yes.

Some of the people in your life are what we might call "pre-converted disciples." They're open. They're asking questions. They feel something stirring, but they're not ready to make a decision—and that's okay. They need time. They need consistency. They need someone who doesn't disappear after one spiritual conversation. They need relationship.

As Alan Hirsch says in *Disciplism,*

> We need to reconceive discipleship as a process that includes pre-conversion discipleship and post-conversion discipleship. A person's salvation really is God's business, isn't it? Our part in it is to simply devote meaningful time and commitment to making disciples of whoever wants to share the journey with us—as we go.[4]

Theologian and church historian Leonard Sweet describes evangelism not as pressure or persuasion, but as "nudging," when he states, "evangelism is nudging people to pay attention to the mission of God in their lives and to the necessity of responding to that initiative in ways that birth new realities and the new birth."[5] Nudging people to pay attention to the ways God is already at work in their lives. Nudging them to connect the dots. Nudging them toward love, grace, hope, and truth. And that can't be rushed.

In this kind of friendship, you don't need to have all the answers. You don't need a polished presentation. You just need to show up with presence, compassion, and a willingness to stay in the story with them—even if the journey is slow. The relational approach recognizes that God's work in a person's life is rarely

Your job isn't to close the deal. It's to walk alongside someone for as long as they'll let you, and trust that God is at work—even when it feels slow, even when there's resistance, even when you're not sure it's going anywhere.

a single quick event, but an ongoing process. That means your job isn't to close the deal. It's to walk alongside someone for as long as they'll let you, and trust that God is at work—even when it feels slow, even when there's resistance, even when you're not sure it's going anywhere.

And here's the beauty of it: God isn't just doing something in them. He's doing something in you, too. When you commit to walking with someone else—whether they're already following Jesus or just starting to wonder about him—you'll find yourself being shaped in the process. That's what makes discipleship so powerful. It's not one-sided. It's mutual. We grow together.

Jesus didn't say, "Go into the world and get people to raise their hands." He said, "Go and make disciples." That takes time. It takes patience. But it's worth it. Because when someone comes to know Jesus through relationship—not pressure or performance—they often become the kind of disciple who does the same for others.

Relationships Aren't a Program; They're a Shared Life

If you've ever met Brian, you know he's the real deal. No hype, no platform, just someone who bleeds evangelship—the kind of disciple-maker who lives it out loud in the most ordinary but powerful ways.

While most people barbecue in their backyards to keep things private, Brian grills on the *front porch*. Literally. He sets up in front of his house so the neighbors can walk up, grab a burger, and stay awhile. No sign-up sheets. No outreach flyers. Just open doors, good food, and real conversation.

It's no surprise then that one of Brian's most impactful disciple-making stories began not at a church event or conference but on a basketball court in Little Village—*at midnight*—on New Year's Eve.

Back in 2005, Brian was invited to play late-night hoops with some friends. One of them brought a seventeen-year-old named Preston. Preston didn't grow up in church. No Sunday School. No Vacation Bible School. Just a sharp kid from the neighborhood trying to find his way.

That night, Brian's friend nudged him and said, "Hey, share your story with Preston." So he shared his testimony about how God showed up in his life and transformed him. Nothing flashy. Just honest. Real. Relational. That brief interaction planted a seed.

Fast-forward a couple years—Brian was at a Christian event and saw a young man performing spoken-word poetry on stage. It was Preston. But this time, something was different. His poetry had changed. It was full of truth. Gospel truth.

Afterward, Brian pulled him aside: "What happened, man?"

Turns out, Preston had given his life to Jesus sometime after their first encounter. The seed had sprouted. But there was a gap— he wasn't deeply connected to a church. He was being handed a mic but hadn't yet been handed the depth of life-on-life discipleship.

That's when Brian stepped in again.

They started meeting regularly. Reading Scripture. Asking hard questions. Eating meals. Laughing. Sharing real life—the kind that isn't confined to one-hour sessions at a coffee shop. The kind that includes late-night texts, spontaneous hangouts, and showing up when life gets messy.

They discipled each other around the table. Around the fire pit. Around the rhythms of everyday life—evangelship.

Over the next decade, Preston became a leader in their house church. He got married. Had four kids. And eventually moved to Atlanta. But the relationship didn't fade.

Their connection shifted—in the same way it did for Jesus when he told his disciples, "I no longer call you servants.... Instead, I have called you friends" (John 15:15).

That's what Preston and Brian became. Still learning. Still growing. Still calling each other for prayer, for wisdom, or just to hang out. They've gone on mission trips together, vacations, conferences. And whenever they're in the same city, they don't miss a beat. It's a brotherhood now.

Too often, we treat discipleship like a task on a to-do list. But what if it's more like friendship on purpose? What if the most powerful moments happen not in a Bible study but in the everyday stuff—on a porch, at a gym, or while grabbing tacos? These small, consistent acts may not win applause or fill a stadium, but they are the ground where real, lasting faith takes root.

Evangelship Is About Roots, Not Just Results

We live in a world obsessed with going viral.

We measure our worth by likes, follows, views, influence. Even in ministry, we're tempted to think big = better. That if we're not seeing quick results or building something visible, we're somehow not doing enough.

But Jesus didn't teach that. He talked about seeds. He talked about mustard-sized faith. Hidden yeast. Slow-growing trees. He was never impressed by crowds; he was moved by the faithfulness of the few. Because the kingdom doesn't grow on a stage. It grows in the dirt.

If Jesus were alive today in human form, most of us would probably tell him to build a platform.

"Start a podcast."

"Go live."

"Write a book."

But when we look at how Jesus operated, we don't see a numbers game. He didn't try to reach as many people as fast as possible. He had thousands of followers, sure—but he chose twelve to walk closely with. And even among the Twelve, he pulled Peter, James, and John in even closer. Not for exclusivity but for depth.

He walked with them, ate with them, corrected them, believed in them—and then left the future of the world in their hands.

Jesus' model wasn't mass production—it was *relationship*.

The gospel spread not because Jesus went viral but because he went deep.

And if you've been trying to reach the masses while ignoring the one God put right in front of you, maybe it's time to go back to the dirt.

> *The gospel spread not because Jesus went viral but because he went deep.*

Let me tell you about Alma.

She led a women's prayer group for decades. Never more than five or six ladies. They'd meet, pray, read Scripture, cry, and intercede for their church and neighborhood.

One of those women led her son to Christ.

That son became a pastor.

That pastor planted a church in a city that hadn't seen gospel growth in years.

And that church? It planted five more.

All because Alma sowed quietly. In dirt. Week after week.

Nobody clapped.

Nobody posted it.

But heaven saw it—and the fruit is still growing.

Let's get practical. What does it mean to live a life of growing roots, not just results?

Sow, even when you don't see fruit. Discipleship is messy. Some people walk away. Some take years to respond. Some won't bloom until long after you're gone. But sow anyway. "Those who sow with tears will reap with songs of joy" (Psalm 126:5).

Don't prioritize speed over formation. Sometimes the most fruitful relationships are the quietest and the slowest. You're not failing—you're forming. Jesus spent the majority of his three years of ministry investing in just twelve people, knowing that their widespread impact would only begin after his departure.

Dig deep before you grow wide. Before you start another Bible study, build another team, or launch a ministry, ask: "Have I gone deep with the few God has already given me?" Depth creates durability. And durability creates legacy.

The Power of a Small Victory

We've all heard the phrase, "It's the little things that count." And when it comes to evangelship, nothing could be truer.

Most people don't drop everything and give their life to Jesus in one dramatic moment. For the vast majority of us, faith is a slow, steady unfolding—a journey made up of small steps and quiet victories. It takes time. It takes trust. And it takes friendships with purpose—someone willing to walk alongside us through it all.

If you want to be that kind of person—someone who shows up, stays the course, and helps others grow—there's something simple and powerful you need to remember: Celebrate the wins. Big or small. Seen or unseen. Celebrate them.

Sometimes the most meaningful milestones don't look like

much on the surface. Maybe your disciple had their first real conversation about Jesus with a friend. Maybe they prayed out loud for the first time. Maybe they opened their Bible on their own or showed kindness to someone they usually struggle with. To them, it might feel like no big deal. But to you? It's a moment to pause and say, *This matters.*

When you notice and celebrate those moments, you're affirming that their growth is real—that their effort is seen. You're showing them that transformation doesn't have to be flashy to be worth celebrating. It's often the smallest shifts that signal the deepest change.

And when those victories come? Don't keep them quiet. Celebrate them together.

Tell others in your circle what God is doing. Let the person you're discipling know their progress is worth shouting about. It builds community. It builds courage. It helps them see their story is part of something much bigger than themselves.

A small win for one person is a ripple for many. It stirs hope. It stirs momentum. And it reminds everyone watching that God is moving—even in the quiet, slow, in-between spaces.

So don't wait for perfection. Celebrate progress.

Because evangelship isn't about arriving—it's about continuing. And every step forward is worth celebrating.

Every single one.

> *Evangelship isn't about arriving—it's about continuing. And every step forward is worth celebrating.*

The Power of Patience

People are going to stumble. They're going to resist. They're going to grow more slowly than you hoped.

And you're going to feel it.

You'll wonder if you're wasting your time. You'll feel the weight of praying with no visible progress. You'll be tempted to back off.

But don't.

Sticking with someone and continuing to build relationship through the awkwardness, the doubts, the missteps—that's where the deepest growth happens. That's when your faithfulness starts to mean something beyond words. Your presence, your consistency, your patience—it all adds up.

Growth doesn't come in straight lines. But with time, and grace, and a lot of little nudges forward, you'll start to see the fruit.

- -

Reflection and Intention
Chapter Summary: Building Friendships of Purpose

- Real transformation rarely comes from *one spectacular moment*—it grows through *steady presence and faithful friendship*.

- Jesus began not with sermons or spectacle, but with *presence*—asking for water at a well, inviting conversation, meeting people as *equals* in their shared humanity.

- Evangelship *isn't a transaction or a program*. It's two thirsty people *walking toward Jesus together*. It's not about hierarchy—expert and beginner—but *friendship on purpose*, shaped by grace.

- Genuine relationships take *time, attention, and vulnerability*. They grow through listening, through shared meals, through laughter and tears. Jesus didn't call his disciples servants. He called them *friends*.

- *Discipleship is not just about the destination but the journey.* Every step toward Jesus—no matter how small—is worth recognizing.

- *Consistency is the soil where trust is built,* where seeds planted long ago are watered, and where God's unseen work takes root.

- The call is simple but radical: *Show up,* again and again, *trusting God* with the fruit.

- *Small wins* often build the foundation for lasting transformation. Ignoring them can discourage growth; *naming them can spark momentum.*

Reflection Questions: A Personal Assessment

Take a moment to reflect on these questions—they're meant to help you notice where steady presence, intentional friendship, and small wins are shaping the people around you.

- When you think about your current relationships, do you tend to treat people as "projects" or as friends? What's the difference? What would it look like to practice "friendship with purpose" with them this week?

- How well do you practice listening—not to fix, but to truly nurture relationships? What step could you take to grow in this?

- Who in your life has most impacted you through consistent presence rather than big moments? What did their consistency teach you?

- Do you tend to focus more on what still needs to change rather than what God has already done? Why?

- Think of someone you're discipling or encouraging right now—what's one small victory you can affirm in them?
- Who in your circle is open but "not ready yet"? How can you commit to walking with them without pressure or rushing?
- What would it take for you to slow down enough to cultivate a relationship that lasts beyond programs, seasons, or agendas?
- What specific practice can you adopt this week to intentionally celebrate progress in yourself or others?

Breath Prayer

As you build relationships this week, pause and pray:

Inhale: *Lord, give me patience.*
Exhale: *Help me to be present.*

part three

MAINTAIN THE MOVEMENT

9

walk together

If you want to go fast, go alone. If you want to go far, go together.

African Proverb

LET'S NAME SOMETHING hard: We are more connected than ever ... and more alone than ever.

We have endless followers, friends, and feeds—yet real friendship, especially among Christians on mission, feels rare.

But if evangelship is going to be more than a short burst of effort, we can't do it in isolation. We weren't designed to carry the mission of Jesus solo. We were made to do it with one another.

Daniel Didn't Stand Alone

I love to tell the story of Daniel in the lions' den. But before Daniel ever stood alone in that pit ... he stood with his people in the fire of exile.

In Daniel 1–3, we meet the crew: Daniel, Hananiah, Mishael, and Azariah (better known as Shadrach, Meshach, and Abednego). These weren't just classmates in Babylon—they were brothers in the faith.

They trained together. They resisted cultural compromise together. They prayed for God's wisdom together. And when the heat got turned up—literally—they were thrown into the fire together. And the most beautiful part? God didn't show up before the fire—he walked with them in it (Daniel 3:24–25). That's the gift of gospel-centered community. Not escape from the fire—but courage in the middle of it.

You Can't Fight Babylon Alone

Let's be honest: Our Western culture pushes independence hard.

"Do your own thing."

"Build your own brand."

"Protect your own space."

But Babylon was never meant to be faced alone. Neither is your neighborhood, your workplace, or your calling.

Dietrich Bonhoeffer, writing in Nazi Germany, knew a thing or two about exile. And he knew that discipleship requires community—especially when culture gets dark. A theme he weaves throughout his book *Life Together* is that the Christian life is personal but never private. Bonhoeffer knew we were made to walk together.[1]

I heard a story of a man named Elijah who started a men's Bible study in his garage. Nothing fancy. Just lawn chairs, cheap pizza, and open Bibles.

At first, it was awkward. Quiet. Safe. But over time? Real conversations started. One man confessed a hidden addiction. Another broke down in tears over a failing marriage. One guy had never prayed out loud in his life—until one night, when he finally did. That garage? It became holy ground. Because it wasn't a program. It was brothers in the fire together.

Here's something more personal: The year was 2002, and I was in the valley.

My wife—my partner of five years—had just gone home to be with the Lord. I was left raising our two-year-old son as a single father, grieving in real time, while trying to lead as a newly appointed English service pastor in the city of Chicago. It was the second year of ministry at Liberty Christian Center, but it felt like I had lost more than I could bear.

I still preached. I still showed up on Sundays. But behind the sermons was a broken man barely holding on. My conversations with God weren't pretty. They were real: "Lord, I'm not happy with you. I know you're real … but I'm not okay with this. I'll preach because I know the Word is true—but I'm not in a good place."

I was surviving. But I was not thriving. And deep down … I was ready to quit.

Three Men and a Game of Bones

About a year into my grief, I got a call that one of my college buddies was getting married. The guys were throwing a bachelor party at a bar and grill owned by a friend of ours. And to be honest? I was *this close* to going.

I thought, *Maybe I'll meet someone. Maybe this will lift the fog. Maybe this ministry life isn't for me after all.*

So I got dressed—sharp. Ready to head out. Ready to put my grief on pause. Ready to stop being the "pastor" for just one night.

And that's when it happened.

As I opened the front door, there they were: three of my closest friends—all pastors—standing on my porch with a box of dominoes in hand.

One of them grinned and said, "Larry, we're here to cheer you up, bro. Let's play some bones!"

Now if you're Puerto Rican, you know what time it is. Dominoes isn't a game. It's an *event*. It's loud. It's sacred. It's home.

I figured they'd be gone in a couple of hours or so—they all had church the next day, after all. The bar scene wasn't going anywhere. So we sat down and let the bones hit the table.

Around midnight, one of them asked, "Hey man ... why you dressed like that?"

I hesitated. "Oh, uh ... just trying out my outfit for church tomorrow."

They didn't press. They just kept playing.

They just stayed.

Until 1 a.m.

As they were getting ready to leave, one of them turned at the door and said something that still echoes in my soul: "Larry—you are not alone, bro. God has more for you than you know. Stay focused. Stay the course."

Then they laid hands on me and prayed.

And when the door shut behind them, I dropped to my knees and wept.

They were my Shadrach, Meshach, and Abednego.

That night, they didn't just play dominoes—they stood in the fire with me.

> *Evangelship isn't a solo mission. It's a shared one.*

They reminded me that evangelship isn't a solo mission. It's a shared one. As Hebrews 10:24 encourages, "Let us consider how we may spur one another on toward love and good deeds."

If they hadn't shown up that night, I might have walked away from everything. But God used their presence to breathe courage back into my lungs.

The Brotherhood That Kept Growing

Today, that brotherhood has grown to many more. I have friends I can talk to about anything. What we've formed is a brotherhood of no judgment—but also no compromise. A space where we can be real, raw, and honest ... but also call each other higher. We rebuke when we need to. We encourage constantly. We hold each other to the standard—not just of being better men or better husbands, but better followers of Jesus.

This is the kind of community that holds up your arms when you're too weak to lift them.

This is evangelship.

Bonhoeffer reminds us that spiritual friendship isn't a luxury for Christian life—it's a lifeline. In *Life Together*, he says, "The physical presence of other Christians is a source of incomparable joy and strength to the believer."[2] True friendship in Christ isn't optional for kingdom people; it's part of how we experience and extend God's grace to one another.

You never know when your "showing up" is someone else's salvation from despair.

One game of dominoes turned into a divine intervention.

Three friends with no platform became pastoral lifelines.

> *You never know when your "showing up" is someone else's salvation from despair.*

One word of encouragement rerouted a future.

That's the power of "one anothering."[3]

Building Gospel Community That Sustains the Mission

If you want to live a life of evangelship for the long haul, here are four essentials of community that will carry you through:

Proximity over performance. "We were delighted to share with you not only the gospel of God but our lives as well" (1 Thessalonians 2:8). You don't need a polished group. You need a present one that knows the real you. The strength for evangelship comes from life-on-life honesty within community.

Mutual encouragement over lone heroism. "Let us consider how we may spur one another on towards love and good deeds" (Hebrews 10:24–25). No one in the New Testament discipled or evangelized alone. Even Paul had Barnabas, Silas, Timothy, and countless "co-laborers." Community isn't about becoming individual experts—it's about becoming like Jesus *together*.

Honesty over hype. "But he said to me, 'My grace is sufficient for you, for my power is made perfect in weakness.' Therefore I will boast all the more gladly about my weaknesses, so that Christ's power may rest on me" (2 Corinthians 12:9). Real community isn't built on pretending. Your group doesn't need your highlight reel—they need your heart and the truth about where you need God's strength and their support.

Mission over maintenance. "Two are better than one … If either of them falls down, one can help the other up" (Ecclesiastes 4:9–10). Christian community isn't just about safety. It's about *sending* and *being sent*. The fire doesn't just burn brighter together—it spreads when we go together.

What If You Don't Have That Yet?

Some of you may be thinking, *I don't have people like that.*

First—*pray for them.* Ask God to send you one or two brothers or sisters who will walk with you in mission and formation.

Second—*be that person* for someone else. Start the text thread, open your door, and make the invite.

Sometimes the community you long for is waiting to be built through your vulnerability and initiation.

So take the time to reflect on the following:

- Who's walking with you?
- Who are you checking in on—even at midnight?
- Who needs to hear today: "You're not alone"?

Evangelship is not just about reaching the world. It's about refusing to let your brother or sister go silent in the dark. It's not always fire from a pulpit—sometimes it's healing at the kitchen table. Let your friendships preach. Let your presence carry weight. Let your community become the living altar where others can collapse safely.

. . . .

Reflection and Intention
Chapter Summary: Walking Together

- *Discipleship and evangelism are not solo missions.* God designed his people to live, serve, and grow together.
- True gospel-centered community provides *courage, accountability,* and *sustenance* in the fire of life.
- *Proximity, mutual encouragement, honesty,* and *mission* are the pillars of a Christian community that lasts.
- *Show up for others.* Your presence, prayers, and authentic friendship can be a lifeline when someone is struggling—even if it looks as simple as a game of dominoes.

Reflection Questions: A Personal Assessment
Let these questions help you recognize the people God has placed in your life and how you can show up for them faithfully, even in small everyday ways.

- Who are the people currently walking with you in faith? Are they providing encouragement, accountability, and presence?
- Have you experienced a moment where someone's presence or friendship made a difference in your spiritual life? How did it shape you?
- In what ways are you actively "showing up" for others—beyond church programs or official roles?
- Are there relationships you need to initiate or invest in to create a stronger community around you?
- How can you be a source of courage, honesty, and mission for someone else in their journey of faith?

Breath Prayer

As you enter spaces of community and relationship this week, stop and invite the Spirit:

> **Inhale:** *Lord, help me walk with others in faith.*
> **Exhale:** *Let my presence bring courage, hope, and love.*

10

persevere in hard seasons

The cross is the symbol of death, and it stands at the very heart of the Gospel. If our discipleship does not look like death to self in the hard seasons, then it is not the discipleship of Christ.

Elisabeth Elliot

EVANGELSHIP ISN'T ALWAYS a highlight reel. More often, it's quiet, unseen faithfulness in the middle of hard, confusing, or even painful moments. It's walking with people not just through their breakthroughs, but through their breakdowns. And if Jesus— the Son of God himself—had a wilderness, a Gethsemane, and a Judas, we shouldn't expect the path of following him (or helping others follow him) to look any different.

These hard seasons aren't just for the ones we're discipling; they are tools God uses to forge our character, too. These moments aren't detours. They are part of the journey. And in many ways, they are where the deepest formation and perseverance happen.

Jesus didn't stumble into the wilderness. Scripture tells us he was "led by the Spirit" into it (Luke 4:1). Let that sink in. God brought him there on purpose.

The wilderness isn't about punishment. It's about preparation. It's where identity is tested. It's where endurance is refined. And maybe hardest of all—it's where God is often silent.

But silence isn't absence. The Spirit was with Jesus, even when no one else was. And he is with us, too.

As disciple-makers, we have to resist the urge to rescue people out of their wilderness. It's not our job to fix it. Our job is to be present in it. Sometimes that looks like prayer. Sometimes that looks like showing up with a meal. Sometimes it's just sitting with them in the silence.

We can't carry someone else's cross. But we can walk beside them as they remember the One who already has.

I'll never forget the winter of 2002. My first wife was rushed to the hospital, and before I knew it, she was placed on a respirator. In the midst of the chaos, I called my pastor and mentor, Pastor Pla, who lived all the way in New Jersey. When I told him what was happening, he asked quietly, "Larry, do you want me to come to Chicago to be with you?" I said, "I'd love that, Pastor, but I know you're busy." The next day, he was standing by my side.

That week felt like walking through fire. Everyone meant well—they told me to have faith, to believe for a miracle, to keep hoping. But no one wanted to say the one thing my heart feared most. Pastor Plá did. One afternoon, as the machines hummed beside us, he asked, "Larry, do you believe Jesus can heal your wife?" "Yes," I said without hesitation. He nodded and then gently asked, "And what if he doesn't? Are you ready to face that?"

Tears welled up in my eyes. I looked at him and blurted out,

"I hate you, but I love you. If I have to let her go, I will." He just smiled, knowing my pain, and said, "I know you love me, and I'm glad you can see the bigger picture." Then he hugged me, prayed with me, and didn't leave my side for almost two weeks—until we laid my wife to rest.

Pastor Pla chose to stand beside me in my darkest valley. He allowed me to mourn. He sat with me in what felt like my own Gethsemane. He persevered with me, and his perseverance helped me to persevere.

Pastor Pla didn't try to fix my pain; he shared it. Pastor and author Paul David Tripp captures this so well when he writes, "You are most loving, patient, kind, and gracious when you are aware that there is no truth that you could give to another that you don't desperately need yourself."[1]

We're not trying to be someone's savior; we're trying to be present enough to remind them that the Savior is already there. Presence doesn't rescue—it restores. It doesn't solve—it stands. It's in those sacred spaces of shared pain that perseverance is born and hope is renewed.

Gethsemane: The Agony Before the Assignment

Gethsemane wasn't just a place of prayer. It was a place of crushing.

Jesus, overwhelmed with sorrow, begged his friends to stay awake and pray. But they slept. He asked the Father to take the cup from him. But heaven stayed quiet. He sweat blood.

This is what obedience sometimes looks like. And if you've ever found yourself in a season where you feel alone in your calling or crushed under the weight of what you know you're supposed to do—you're not crazy. You're just in Gethsemane.

And Gethsemane is sacred ground.

The grape must be pressed to produce wine. The soul must be tested to carry resurrection power.

If you're walking with someone in their garden moment, don't rush them through it. Remind them they're not abandoned— they're being prepared.

The Betrayal: When Judas Shows Up

And then, there's the betrayal.

Not everyone who starts the journey with you will stay. Sometimes, the deepest wounds come not from the outside, but from the ones we thought we could trust.

Jesus had his Judas. And sooner or later, we'll encounter ours, too.

Here's the uncomfortable truth: Judas' kiss didn't stop Jesus' mission. It set it into motion. Sometimes betrayal is the very thing that moves us into the next phase of God's call on our lives.

> *Sometimes betrayal is the very thing that moves us into the next phase of God's call on our lives.*

This doesn't make it easier. It still hurts. But we can walk through it without becoming bitter. We can teach others how to face betrayal with grace. We can be the ones who keep showing up, even when it would be easier to disappear.

Because the goal isn't just survival—it's formation.

When It Hurts Too Much to Keep Going—But You Do Anyway

Let's be real. Ministry isn't neat. Discipleship, at times, can leave scars on your heart. And when you're in it for the long

haul—loving, walking with, praying for, pouring into someone—
it doesn't feel like a job. It feels like family.

But here's something that will set you free: You don't own
the people you disciple. They don't belong to you. They belong to
Jesus.

That truth sounds good on paper until life flips it on you.

I learned this the hard way through a young man I'll never
forget. His name was Julio.

Julio was gifted—an incredible man, a former professional
soccer player turned coach who oversaw a league with over four
hundred student-athletes. He was strong, passionate, and loved
Jesus. And I had a front-row seat to disciple him.

He wasn't just a project. He was a brother.

He'd call late at night just to pray. We talked about everything—life, struggles, jealousy, and heartbreak. Especially after his
engagement fell apart, he wrestled deeply with anger. But he always
reached out … until the one night I couldn't answer.

I was away, speaking at a conference. My phone rang, and I
missed it.

That night, I came home to news that shattered me. Julio had
come looking for me at the church, and when he didn't find me, he
left. Later that evening, I got the call: He was at the hospital. He
had taken his own life.

I'll never forget standing in my kitchen, frozen, phone in hand,
blaming myself.

"How did I not see this?"

"Why didn't I call back sooner?"

It broke me.

But in that grief, the Lord whispered something I needed to
hear:

"He was mine before he was yours."

As painful as it is to admit, we are not saviors. We're not supposed to carry the weight of someone else's soul. Jesus already did that on the cross. These are the moments that hit you in the gut. You replay the conversations. You second-guess the silences. You wonder if more prayer, more presence, more something could have made a difference.

But this is where evangelship gets gritty. It's not just about pouring into others. It's about being poured out. As scholar and pastor Henri Nouwen reminds us, "We are not the healers, we are not the reconcilers, we are not the givers of life."[2] Our calling is to let our limited love become a doorway for the unlimited love of God, not to replace him.

The apostle Paul says it like this in 2 Timothy 4:6: "For I am already being poured out like a drink offering." This pouring out is part of the process; it's not to destroy or stop us, but it plays a role in purification and preparation. Paul says it best in 2 Corinthians 4:7–9:

> But we have this treasure in jars of clay, to show that this all-surpassing power is from God and not from us. We are hard pressed on every side, but not crushed; perplexed, but not in despair; persecuted, but not abandoned; struck down, but not destroyed.

These painful truths aren't shared to discourage you. They're here to prepare you. So that you are equipped to live the life of a disciple-maker. Because evangelship isn't always pretty. Sometimes the ones you love most don't make it. And that doesn't mean you failed. It just means you're human.

So what do we do?

We show up anyway.

We keep praying anyway.

We keep listening anyway.

We keep trusting that God is doing more than we can see.

Jesus didn't call us to produce perfect outcomes. He called us to be faithful witnesses.

So if you're reading this and you've lost someone you discipled … if the weight of "what if" is crushing your soul … let me say this to you like I wish someone had said to me: You were never meant to be their savior. You were called to be their companion.

And in the mystery of God's grace, sometimes your presence was more powerful than you'll ever know.

Let the pain shape you. Let it teach you. And then—get back in the game.

> *Let the pain shape you. Let it teach you. And then—get back in the game.*

Because someone else needs you to show up tomorrow.

Evangelship isn't just about what God is doing in someone else—it's also about what he's doing in you. These moments of wilderness, agony, and betrayal aren't just part of their story. They're part of yours, too. They are the tools God uses to refine, to reveal, and to prepare.

You are called. You are chosen. And yes—even in the fire—you are being proven faithful.

Reflection and Intention
Chapter Summary: Persevering in Hard Seasons

- Discipleship in hard seasons is often *quiet, unseen, and emotionally demanding.*
- The *wilderness* tests *identity* and *endurance*; *Gethsemane* stretches *obedience* and *trust*; *betrayal* challenges *faithfulness* and *grace.*

- *Presence matters more than outcomes*—we cannot carry others' souls, but we can walk with them *faithfully.*
- *Hard seasons refine both the disciple and the disciple-maker,* shaping character, empathy, and perseverance.
- Faithful accompaniment requires *trusting God* to work beyond what we see or control.

Reflection Questions: A Personal Assessment

Before moving on, let these questions create space for honest reflection, helping you name where you are on the journey and how God is shaping you through the weight of this season.

- Which part of the journey are you in right now—wilderness, Gethsemane, or betrayal?
- How do you respond when God feels silent?
- Are you trying to carry people on your own strength, or are you trusting Jesus to do the saving?
- Who around you needs your quiet faithfulness right now?
- How has a hard season shaped your character or deepened your trust in God?

Breath Prayer

As you pause to breathe, allow this simple prayer to steady your heart, reminding you that perseverance is not powered by your strength but sustained by God's presence:

Inhale: *Jesus, I cannot do this alone.*
Exhale: *I trust you with these lives.*

11

shoot every arrow

[Claiming every sector of public life for Christ] will only happen when local congregations renounce an introverted concern for their own life, and recognize that they exist for the sake of those who are not members, as sign, instrument, and foretaste of God's redeeming grace for the whole life of society.

Lesslie Newbigin

IN NAVY SEAL training, there's a bell that sits in the middle of the courtyard. Every recruit sees it. Everyone knows what it means. If the cold, the exhaustion, or the pressure becomes too much, you can walk up, ring the bell, and quit. No more long runs. No more freezing water. No more being pushed beyond what you thought you could handle.

But every instructor warns them: "That bell will whisper your name. But if you want to make a difference—don't you dare ring it."

The ones who make it through aren't always the fastest or the strongest. They're the ones who want it the most. The ones who choose desire over comfort, hunger over ease, purpose over quitting.

At its core, isn't that a perfect picture of following Jesus? Not the polished version. Not the Sunday version. Not the "I'm fine, thank you" version. The real version. The version where faith costs you something. The version where you feel like giving up. The version where the bell is whispering your name.

Living out evangelship—living as someone who reflects Jesus and helps others walk toward him—will eventually bring you to that bell. And in those moments, there's a question you have to answer for yourself: How bad do I want it?

Not "How gifted am I?" Not "How spiritual do I feel?" Not "How perfect is my Christian life?" It's about hunger. It's about desire. It's about the refusal to ring the bell.

Jesus himself wondered aloud: "When the Son of Man comes, will he find faith on the earth?" (Luke 18:8). He wasn't questioning if he'd find churches. Or worship sets. Or conferences. He was asking if he'd still find hunger.

The Quiet Drift of a Tired Generation

If we're honest, these last few years since the pandemic have been marked by isolation, division, and uncertainty. And it's shaken people to the core. Some have walked away from church. Some have walked away from hope. Some have quietly walked away from faith. Jesus said this would happen: "Many will turn away from the faith…. the love of most will grow cold" (Matthew 24:10, 12). Paul warned us too: "Some will abandon the faith" (1 Timothy 4:1).

Evangelship isn't hype. It isn't a strategy. It isn't a program. It's the ordinary, everyday decision not to quit.

These verses aren't meant to scare us. They're meant to wake us up. Because this is the moment where evangelship matters the most. Evangelship isn't hype. It isn't a strategy. It isn't a program. It's the ordinary, everyday decision not to quit.

Not to quit on God. Not to quit on people. Not to quit on the mission. Not to quit on the work he started inside you.

It's living the way Lesslie Newbigin, the missionary theologian, defined the church's task—as a "sign, instrument, and foretaste of God's redeeming grace"[1]—a person whose faith keeps shining when others burn out. It's choosing hunger over quitting.

Hunger Beats Talent Every Time

When my youngest son turned fourteen, a few people spoke over him that God would use him in school. And a year later, at fifteen, he was suddenly chosen to lead his school Christian club. He didn't ask or campaign for it—the opportunity found him.

Curious, I asked him after his first meeting, "So, what did you actually do?"

He shrugged, a little embarrassed. "I taught Mark 5. You always said it works when you don't know what to say."

I laughed because he was right. I hadn't told him directly, but he'd overheard me jokingly telling colleagues, "When in doubt, Mark 5 always works!"

But the real lesson here is how simple evangelship can be. God opens doors we don't expect, and we step through them with whatever we have.

Then my son said something that hit deeper. He had the other students watch an Alpha video from a series I'd introduced him to weeks before. And then they prayed together a prayer of salvation. But he told me, "Dad, I feel like I missed the opportunity to explain more to them about salvation. I'm not sure they knew what they were praying."

So I shared with him about how following Jesus is a journey, not a moment. A process, not a formula. A relationship, not a slogan.

Then I asked him, "How many prayed?"

"Eleven," he said quietly.

In my head, I shouted, *Eleven?! This is amazing!*

My shyest kid. The quietest one in the house. The one who tries to stay away from standing out. And God used him—not because he was loud, not because he was confident, but because he was willing. Hunger beats talent every time.

The Story of the Arrows

There's a story in the Bible about a king named Jehoash and an old prophet named Elisha (2 Kings 13:14–19). Elisha is dying. The end is close. The man who once healed a leper, multiplied oil, raised the dead, and mentored kings is now frail and weak.

Jehoash, a complicated king, visits him. He respects the prophet but doesn't really follow God with his whole heart (2 Kings 13:11). Elisha gives him one final instruction: "Take the arrows.… Strike the ground" (v.18). Jehoash obeys—kind of. He hits the ground three times and stops. And Elisha gets upset. Not because Jehoash disobeyed. But because he stopped too soon.

He quit before the breakthrough. He gave effort but not hunger. He struck—but not with fire. And the prophet tells him plainly: "You should have struck the ground five or six times" (v.19). In other words: "You should've wanted it more." You can feel the weight of that story if you sit with it long enough. It's the tragedy of *almost*.

Of *good enough.*

Of *getting tired in the middle of a miracle.*

Of *stopping because it's easier to quit than to keep going.*

It's the sound of a man who didn't ring the bell—he just

quietly walked away from the arrows. Half-hearted striking results in half-completed victories.

> *Half-hearted striking results in half-completed victories.*

Why This Story Matters for You

Every one of us has a moment where we feel like Jehoash. Moments where we're tired. Where prayers feel repetitive. Where people disappoint us. Where God feels silent. Where life feels heavy. Where striking the ground feels pointless.

And the bell starts whispering our name. But disciples who live out evangelship—the everyday ones, not the perfect ones—learn something essential: Breakthrough doesn't come to the ones who quit. It comes to the ones who strike again.

> *Breakthrough doesn't come to the ones who quit. It comes to the ones who strike again.*

Dallas Willard once wrote: "Grace is not opposed to effort; it is opposed to earning."[2] Effort doesn't *save* you. But effort *grows* you. And effort keeps you from quitting when quitting feels reasonable.

That's what evangelship looks like in real life: Showing up again. Praying again. Trying again. Loving again. Believing again. Striking the ground again. Even when you don't feel anything. Even when the results aren't visible. Even when the arrows feel heavy.

Refuse to Die Full

There's a moment in the Elisha story that's easy to miss, but once you see it, you can't unsee it. It's the moment that reveals what happens when we stop striking too soon—when we stop giving, stop pouring, stop investing, stop stretching, stop hungering.

It's a strange, almost cinematic moment right after Elisha dies: A dead man's body is thrown into Elisha's tomb and touches Elisha's bones—and the man comes back to life (2 Kings 13:20–21). Just picture that. Elisha was one of the most anointed men in the Old Testament, but when he died, something surprising happened: The anointing didn't die with him … it stayed in his bones. There was still that much power in him. Still that much potential. Still that much anointing. It was just unused.

Something he never passed on.

Something he never released.

Something that should've lived beyond him but didn't.

And that reality forces us to face something simple but sobering: Elisha died full. Not empty. But full!

Full of unspent potential.

Full of unused arrows.

Full of an anointing that never transferred.

Maybe his excuse was that he didn't see the same hunger in the next generation that he had for Elijah's double portion (2 Kings 2:9). Elijah threw his mantle on Elisha (1 Kings 19:19), but Elisha never threw his mantle on anyone. And that's tragic. Because the next generation was waiting. The nation was desperate. The world needed another voice. But the arrows stayed in the quiver.

Here's the truth no one likes to admit: A believer who dies full lived safe. A believer who dies empty lived surrendered.

A disciple who refuses to pour into others becomes a reservoir instead of a river.

A church that doesn't pass on its anointing dies with its arrows still in its hand. A disciple who refuses to pour into others becomes a reservoir instead of a river. And evangelship—real, everyday, live-it-out faith—refuses that option.

It chooses hunger.

It chooses desire.

It chooses to pour everything out.

And for the everyday follower of Jesus—for you—this becomes a quiet, gentle warning: *Don't let your anointing die with you.* Don't bury your arrows. Don't leave your impact unspent—not as individuals, not as families, not as churches.

Don't Die with Your Arrows in Your Hand

A while ago, my wife, daughter, and I were on a college campus tour at DePaul University in Chicago. One professor mentioned that they often take students to Graceland Cemetery, the final resting place of some of the city's most influential figures: Marshall Field, George Pullman, Daniel Burnham. The students listen to the stories of these individuals at their tombs and write papers about their lives. These were innovators, architects, industrialists—people who shaped cities and economies. But they left absolutely everything behind. Everything.

I couldn't help but think: *The richest place in the world is a cemetery?!* All of us leave our earthly wealth behind, but how many Christians do the same with our calling and influence? How many followers of Jesus die with their arrows still in their hand? How many believers carry gifting, compassion, wisdom, and stories that never made it to the next person? How many disciple-makers remain unborn because someone stopped striking too soon?

So this is where evangelship becomes more than a chapter or a concept. It becomes a conviction: Refuse to die full. Choose to die empty. Pour out everything God placed inside you. Because someone needs what God put

> *Refuse to die full.*
> *Choose to die empty.*
> *Pour out everything*
> *God placed inside you.*

in you. Someone is waiting on the other side of your obedience. Someone's story will change because you kept striking.

A few years ago, I was at a funeral for someone who lived this way—my spiritual father, Pastor Willie. By the end of his life, Alzheimer's had taken many of his memories. But even when his mind faded, his heart for people didn't. He carried around a small booklet with names of people he'd pray for while walking around the neighborhood.

Even when he couldn't remember everything, he remembered the mission.

At his funeral, the stories didn't stop. Person after person talked about how he invested in them, encouraged them, discipled them. His life kept shooting arrows even after he was gone.

And that day, I realized something: The people who make the biggest spiritual impact aren't the ones with the most talent. They're the ones who never stop striking.

> *The people who make the biggest spiritual impact aren't the ones with the most talent. They're the ones who never stop striking.*

Don't Ring the Bell; Don't Stop Striking

There's a moment in Genesis where the patriarch Jacob is dying. He can barely move. But when his son Joseph enters with his grandchildren, Scripture says something powerful: "Israel rallied his strength and sat up" (Genesis 48:2).

Not Jacob. But Israel—meaning that although Jacob's body was failing, his calling and covenantal identity stood up again.[3] Why? Because there was still one more blessing to give. One more generation to speak life into. One more arrow to shoot. This is what it means to carry evangelship.

Not perfection.

Not popularity.

Not spiritual performance.

Just a willingness to say: "I'm not done yet."

Let's bring it all together: You don't need to be the strongest. You don't need to be the smartest. You don't need to have all the answers.

You just need hunger. You just need desire. You just need grit. You just need the courage to try again.

It's the life where you tell yourself: *I will not ring the bell. I will not stop striking. I will not give up on the mission God gave me.* Because the world doesn't need more Christians who quit. It needs people like you and me who keep showing up.

Reflection and Intention
Chapter Summary: Shooting Every Arrow

- Evangelship is *sustained not by talent but by hunger*—the steady refusal to quit even when the bell of discouragement whispers your name.
- God uses the *willing more than the gifted*; availability in simple, everyday moments often becomes the doorway to unexpected influence.
- Jehoash's half-hearted striking exposes a deeper truth: *Partial passion leads to partial victories*—breakthrough belongs to those who keep going.
- Elisha's story warns us not to die full; *unused gifts, unshared wisdom, and unspent anointing are the tragedy of a safe life rather than a surrendered one.*

- *A life poured out becomes a life that multiplies*—our arrows matter because someone's faith, future, or story depends on our obedience.

Reflection Questions: A Personal Assessment

Let these questions guide you into honest reflection, helping you discern where God is calling you to keep striking, keep believing, and keep moving.

- Where do you feel the "bell" whispering your name right now?
- What's one arrow in your hand that you've stopped striking with? Is it prayer? Discipline? Mission? Loving someone difficult?
- What would it look like this week for you to "strike again"— not perfectly but faithfully?
- Whose life might be impacted if you choose not to quit? Who is watching, learning, or listening to your story?
- Where have you settled for partial victory?

Breath Prayer

Allow these breath prayers to anchor you as you recommit to striking your arrows with faith:

Inhale: *I receive your strength for today.*
Exhale: *I release my fear of quitting.*

12

be the event

*Then he said to me, "Prophesy to the breath" ...
and breath entered them; they came to life and
stood up on their feet—a vast army.*

Ezekiel 37:9–10

EZEKIEL STOOD IN a valley full of bones—dry, brittle, lifeless. But when God called him to prophesy, something happened. Not when he analyzed the bones. Not when he just prayed about the bones. But when he opened his mouth—and the breath of God entered the valley.

Evangelship isn't standing on the sidelines explaining life. It's stepping into the valley with your whole being—and allowing the breath of God to flow through you to breathe life into others.

You've read the stories. You've sat in the weight of these truths. You've seen what evangelship can look like—slow, steady, real, rooted, and relational.

But now? It's time to breathe. Because inspiration without incarnation won't raise dry bones. And information without transformation won't make disciples.

God didn't speak directly to the bones at first. He told Ezekiel: "*You* prophesy. *You* speak to the breath. *You* call the wind" (Ezekiel 37:9, my paraphrase).

Sometimes we want God to move without realizing he's waiting to move through us.

Now it's your turn to be the breath for others.

Availability vs. Ability

Early in ministry I learned a quote from one of my mentors that made a lot of sense: "Understanding can wait but obedience can't."

I was just nineteen years old—a young minister full of dreams, zeal, and a heart that genuinely wanted to serve God. But like many young leaders, I was still learning how to discern the *right* thing from the *good* thing.

One evening, I had two options in front of me. The first? A church hangout with a bunch of my Christian friends. You know the kind—laughs, worship music, encouraging conversations, and all-around good vibes. The second? Volunteering at a youth center event at a bowling alley, serving a group of underprivileged, unchurched teenagers. Kids who were rough around the edges. Kids who needed more than just another program—they needed presence. They needed Jesus with skin on.

I was scheduled to go to the bowling alley. I had said yes to the youth center event. But as the day unfolded, I made a quiet shift. I followed what was *comfortable*. I went to the church hangout instead.

The next day, I ran into my mentor and spiritual father, Pastor Choco. If you know him, you know he doesn't waste words. He looked me in the eyes and casually asked, "How was your night?"

I smiled. "It was great! I went to the church event—good people, good conversation."

He nodded, paused, and then with a gentle firmness that only a true father in the faith can carry, he said words I'll never forget. Words that didn't just correct me—they *formed* me.

He said, "Larry, you have a great calling on your life. But let me tell you something. God is not interested in your *ability*. He's interested in your *availability*."

Then he leaned in a little and added, "I've seen God move more in a bowling alley with broken, forgotten kids than I have at a gathering with Christians who are already full."

And just like that, something cracked open in me.

I had missed it. I had missed an opportunity to breathe life into dry bones. But the real twist? *I* was the dry bones. My comfort had cost *me* an encounter. Not just for those kids—but for me.

That moment became an altar in my life. A place of recalibration. A holy confrontation that still speaks to me today.

Have you ever chosen convenience over calling? Have you ever gravitated toward the familiar when God was nudging you toward the forgotten?

This isn't about guilt—it's about *growth*. It's about realizing that ministry doesn't always look like microphones, pulpits, or stages. Sometimes, it looks like a bowling alley. A broken soul. An awkward conversation with someone who doesn't speak your church language. Sometimes, the most sacred spaces are the ones we're tempted to avoid.

As followers of Christ, we must resist the gravitational pull toward what's safe and instead move with courage toward where the Spirit is moving—even if it's messy, inconvenient, or unnoticed.

Here's the truth: God isn't measuring your performance—he's searching for your presence. The kingdom doesn't advance through talent alone. It advances through *availability*. Through showing up when it's easier to stay home. Through loving people who don't always love you back. Through choosing mission over comfort.

Pastor Choco's words were more than a rebuke. They were a prophetic alignment to a principle I now live by—and one I hope you do too:

> *Your greatest usefulness to God is not in what you can do—but in your willingness to go and be present.*

Your greatest usefulness to God is not in what you can do—but in your willingness to go and be present.

B.R.E.A.T.H.—A Lifestyle of Evangelship

Let's look at the story of Ezekiel and consider what it takes to breathe life into people, one letter at a time.

B—Be Present in the Valley

"The hand of the LORD was on me, and he brought me out by the Spirit … and set me in the middle of a valley; it was full of bones" (Ezekiel 37:1).

Ezekiel didn't preach from a distance.

He was placed in the middle of the valley. Evangelship begins with presence. We don't save people from afar—we sit in their ashes, walk their streets, learn their names.

Jesus moved into the neighborhood (John 1:14). So must we.

Ask: *Where has God placed me that feels dry? A workplace? A school? A family line?*

R—Respond to the Spirit's Prompting

"Then he said to me, 'Prophesy to these bones'" (Ezekiel 37:4).

God speaks, and Ezekiel responds. No delay. No overthinking.

Evangelship thrives on obedience in the small moments.

That nudge to text a friend.

That quiet moment to ask, "Can I pray for you?"

That tug to show up again even when you feel invisible.

Ask: *Am I responding to the Spirit … or resisting him?*

E—Encourage Life with Your Words

"Prophesy to these bones and say to them, 'Dry bones, hear the word of the LORD!'" (Ezekiel 37:4).

Your words carry weight.

In a culture full of sarcasm, cynicism, and self-focus, you get to be the one who speaks hope, truth, and life.

We speak the Word, not just opinions.

We call out identity, not just behavior.

We encourage what God is doing—even when others can't see it yet.

"The tongue has the power of life and death" (Proverbs 18:21).

Ask: *What words am I speaking over my valley, my friends, my city?*

A—Abide First, Act Second

"So I prophesied as he commanded me, and breath entered them; they came to life and stood up" (Ezekiel 37:10).

Notice the order in Ezekiel 37:

1. The bones rattle.
2. The bodies form.
3. But they're still not alive until the *breath comes*.

Evangelship is not about hype. It's about *Spirit-filled abiding.*

You can't breathe life you haven't inhaled.

Abide in Christ (John 15).

Let his breath fill you through Scripture, prayer, silence, surrender.

Then move.

You cannot give what you don't possess. So sit at his feet before you walk in his mission.

Ask: *Am I driven by anxiety or rooted in intimacy?*

T—Trust the Process, Not the Pace

"So I prophesied as he commanded me, and breath entered them; they came to life and stood up on their feet—a vast army" (Ezekiel 37:10).

Ezekiel didn't see a full army right away.

First: bones.

Then: sinews.

Then: flesh.

Then: breath.

Then: life.

Then: *an army.*

Evangelship is often *a slow resurrection.* And slow doesn't mean fruitless.

"The kingdom of God is like … a seed" (Mark 4:30–31).

Keep showing up. Keep loving. Keep sowing. God does the resurrecting.

Ask: *Am I willing to stay faithful even when I don't see fast results?*

H—Hold the Vision of a Greater Army

"They … stood up on their feet—a vast army" (Ezekiel 37:10).

What started as dry bones ends as an army.

Evangelship is not about creating better church attenders.

It's about calling dead things to life so they can *rise up and multiply.*

This isn't a personal project. It's a kingdom movement.

Jesus didn't come to make converts. He came to raise up disciples who would carry his life into every corner of the world.

Ask: *Am I just trying to make someone a Christian ... or raise them into a co-laborer?*

A Kingdom Movement

True evangelship means helping the people you invest in become disciple-makers themselves. That's how movements start. That's how the gospel spreads. That's how the kingdom of God grows—through multiplication, not just addition.

Think of it like a wedding. A man and a woman come together and make vows. But those vows don't just shape their relationship—they have ripple effects. Out of that union comes new life, new generations. And that's the heartbeat of evangelship.

When someone says yes to Jesus, it's not the end of their story—it's the beginning of something generational. You're not just walking with them. You're equipping them to walk with others.

One of the clearest examples of this kind of multiplication is the Disciple Making Movement (DMM), which started in Bhojpuri, India, in 1995. The model? Simple but powerful: Don't just make disciples—make disciple-makers.

In DMMs, discipleship starts before someone even decides to follow Jesus. It's what we've been saying throughout these pages: Evangelism and discipleship are not separate activities. DMMs invite people to engage with Scripture, ask honest questions, and take small steps of obedience—even if they're still on the fence about faith. It's not about pressure. It's about process.

Jerry Trousdale, in *Miraculous Movements*, lays out ten key principles that drive this model. A few worth highlighting:

- Go slow at first to go fast later.
- Focus on a few to reach the many.
- Start with creation, not Christ.
- Aim for obedience, not just information.[1]

This approach flips the script. Instead of counting hands raised at the end of a sermon, it builds deep relationships rooted in trust, community, and spiritual discovery. The goal isn't just to get someone "in the door"—it's to help them grow until they open the door for others.

The results speak for themselves. As of 2022, the DMM strategy has led to over two thousand movements worldwide—over 100 million disciples.[2] Many of them haven't even been baptized yet, but they're learning how to follow Jesus and helping others do the same.

Even more powerful? These movements are happening in places once thought "too hard to reach." Muslim-majority nations. Rural communities. Underground churches. DMMs thrive where performance-based evangelism often fail—because they're built on relationships, prayer, and the long game rather than church services, structured programs, and large evangelistic events.

The Great Commission isn't just for the preachers, missionaries, or "super Christians." It's for everyone. Including you.

This Isn't Just for Super Christians

The Great Commission isn't just for the preachers, missionaries, or "super Christians." It's for everyone. Including you.

You don't need a seminary degree to do this. You just need intentionality. Prayer. Curiosity. Consistency. And a willingness to go slow so others can grow deep.

Let me introduce a word you might not use every day: *heuristic*. It means helping someone discover something for themselves. You don't hand them the answer. You walk with them toward it.

Think of evangelship as discipleship rooted in discovery. You're not forcing a message; you're walking with someone until they see Jesus for themselves. Until it clicks. Until the lightbulb turns on.

That's what Jesus did. He didn't just preach at people—he asked questions. He told stories. He led people to their own aha moments. He invited them into a journey where the truth became personal.

Evangelship doesn't spoon-feed people a bunch of answers. It invites them into the mystery. It's slow, messy, relational, and absolutely sacred.

This kind of discipleship can't be boxed into a curriculum. It's a way of living. A mindset. A posture. You basically become the event wherever you are.

Real transformation doesn't come from checklists. It comes from revelation. From people realizing, *Jesus is not just a concept—he's alive, and he's calling me.*

When someone you're discipling has that moment, when they begin to disciple someone else—that's multiplication. That's kingdom movement. That's what it's all about.

Factory Firestarters

For eight years, I had the blessing of working with a group of guys in a factory that made wooden pallets. Now, if you've never been in a factory like that—let me tell you—it's loud, it's sweaty, and the scent of sawdust follows you home. But for me, it became sacred ground. It wasn't a platform, it wasn't a pulpit, but it was a place where evangelship could happen. A place where God could light a fire in the hearts of ordinary men.

Over time, I started gathering some of the guys together before their shift—just to read the Word, share a quick devotional, and pray. It was nothing fancy. Just honest conversation, Scripture, and brotherhood right there in the breakroom or by the punch clock.

There was one guy in particular—Manuel. Big guy. Six-foot-five, towered over most of us. Quiet. Observant. I found out he had been in church before, but for a while now, he'd been drifting—backslidden, as we say. So one day, I pulled him aside during lunch and just asked him, "What do you think about Jesus these days?" And that cracked the door open. He started sharing his story—how he'd grown up in church, how he'd loved it, but never really got involved in anything. He was a benchwarmer in the pews—present but passive.

I invited him to a men's retreat we were hosting. He came, hesitantly at first, but something clicked for him out there. On one of those evenings, while others were getting baptized, he stood up—unprompted—and joined them in the water. It was a holy moment. Not because it was dramatic, but because it was decisive. Manuel was stepping back in.

After that retreat, I began to meet with him regularly— every week, just walking with him, praying, digging into the Word. He eventually brought one of his factory friends to our weekly meetups. That's when the sparks of evangelship started catching fire.

Without any official training, without a curriculum or certificate, Manuel began showing up at the factory at 5 a.m. every morning to pray with the guys before their shift. Nobody told him to. He just did it. Why? Because evangelship is contagious when it's real. He even nudged his friend to lead the prayer one day—passing the torch, just like that.

One morning, I pulled him aside and said, "Manuel, you're doing it. You're leading. You're discipling. Let's take this a step further. Would you be willing to give the devotion next week?"

His face lit up—not with pride, but with purpose. And he did. And it was powerful.

See, evangelship doesn't wait for a title. It celebrates the fruit. It fans into flame the gifts it sees. My job wasn't to micromanage Manuel—it was to make room for him. To celebrate his "yes." Because when a disciple starts making disciples, that's heaven's win column. That's what we live for.

So here's the reminder for us as disciple-makers: When your Manuel starts rising up—don't hold him back, lift him up. Cheer him on. Because evangelship isn't about you being the star—it's about you lighting someone else's match and watching them set the factory floor on fire for Jesus.

. . . .

Reflection and Intention
Chapter Summary: Being the Event

- Evangelship calls us to *step into the valley*—the messy, inconvenient, and unseen places—bringing life where there is dryness.
- Like Ezekiel, we are called to *prophesy to the breath*, allowing God's Spirit to move through our words, presence, and obedience.
- Being "the breath" is about *availability over ability*; it's showing up faithfully, even when no one notices or immediate results aren't visible.

- The B.R.E.A.T.H. framework guides us to:
    - *Be present* where God has placed us.
    - *Respond* promptly to the Spirit's nudges.
    - *Encourage life* through words that carry hope and truth.
    - *Abide first*, acting out of intimacy with Christ.
    - *Trust the process*, even when results are slow.
    - *Hold the vision* of multiplying disciples, not just converts.
- Evangelship is a *kingdom rhythm* of *inhaling God's life* and *exhaling it into the world*, transforming dry bones into an *army*.
- Discipleship is about multiplication, not just conversion. True faith grows when disciples make other disciples.
- Being present, modeling Christ, and guiding others through discovery fosters sustainable spiritual growth.

Reflection Questions: A Personal Assessment

Before you move forward, use these questions to discern how God is inviting you to bring his breath into the dry places around you and to evaluate how faithfully you're living the B.R.E.A.T.H. rhythm.

- Where has God placed you that feels like a "valley" of dry bones?
- How are you responding to the Spirit's nudges in your daily life?
- Are you speaking life and hope with your words, or merely commenting on circumstances?
- Do your actions flow from abiding in Christ, or from anxious striving?

- Are you patient with the pace of God's work, trusting him to resurrect life even when you don't see immediate results?
- Who are the people you are currently discipling, and how are you helping them move toward becoming disciple-makers themselves?
- How can you celebrate and release those you disciple to step into leadership and multiplication?

Breath Prayer

As you pause to breathe, let this prayer center your heart in the Spirit's life-giving presence, reminding you that every act of evangelship begins with receiving his breath:

Inhale: *Spirit of God, fill me with your life.*
Exhale: *I will breathe your life into the world.*

conclusion

be the breath

Let me take you to a moment I'll never forget.

My wife and I had just finished officiating a beautiful wedding for a couple in our church. The ceremony was joyful, the reception elegant. But it was getting late, and since I had to preach the next morning, I asked my wife if she was ready to leave. She said, "Just one more dance—with my dad."

So I waited at the table while she danced, scrolling aimlessly through social media, losing track of time. Suddenly, the lights turned on. Shouts pierced the room. Panic erupted.

I jumped to my feet and ran toward the noise, searching for my wife. That's when I saw her—on the ground, kneeling beside a woman who had collapsed on the dance floor. My wife, a nurse, was performing CPR. One of the brothers of the church was doing the chest compressions, as my wife performed mouth-to-mouth.

Yes, this was post-COVID-19. Yes, we were all still cautious. But she didn't hesitate.

She applied *breath*.

The woman began to vomit. Paramedics rushed in and took over, working on her for over thirty minutes. My wife stood nearby—hands shaking, heart steady. All I could do was watch my wife, in awe of what she just did.

Later that night, as we sat silently at home, we got the call:

"She's alive. The doctor said whoever performed CPR ... saved her life."

My wife had *literally* become the breath. And that, my friend, is exactly what God is asking of *you* and *me*. This generation is gasping for air. People are collapsing emotionally, spiritually, morally, relationally. And the church—*you and I*—have been called not just to preach sermons but to make disciples by *breathing life on the lost.*

Sacred CPR

We cannot have one without the other. Evangelism brings life into people. Discipleship strengthens that breath so they can keep living.

God is calling pastors, leaders, ministers, servants—not just to gather crowds, but to awaken corpses.

He's calling you—not just to inspire, but to *resuscitate.*

To be the breath in a world that's gasping.

So let me ask you … Where is God calling you to *breathe* again? Where have you let discouragement steal your confidence? Where have you allowed betrayal to choke your calling?

Let this chapter be your defibrillator. Let these stories remind you of the sacred CPR God has entrusted to you.

You may be weak. You may be tired. But you still have *breath.* And if you have breath, you still have purpose.

Now go—*be the breath.*

As Paul wrote in 1 Thessalonians 2:8: "Because we loved you so much, we were delighted to share with you not only the gospel of God but our lives as well."

This is evangelship.

acknowledgments

As I reflect on the immense grace it took to bring this book to life, my heart overflows with gratitude. First and foremost, I thank God. Every testimony, every trial, every moment of joy and confusion he allowed me to walk through has shaped the pages of this book. *Evangelship* is not a theory for me—it is the life God has patiently taught me to live. Thank You, Lord, for trusting me with this journey.

To my beautiful wife, Yezenia—you have been my constant companion through every step of this process. Your patience, encouragement, and unwavering love carried me on the days I didn't think I could keep going. Thank you for believing in me, for standing by my side, and for simply being you. *Te amo muchísimo.*

To my incredible children—Caleb, Sadie, Micah, and Jamie—always put God first in everything you do. Chase your calling boldly. His purpose for each of you is extraordinary, and I am honored to be your father.

To my grandsons—Malachi, Noah, and Isaac—I love you boys so much. Never forget who you are in Christ and never stop shining his light.

To my mother, Carmen Perez—I know you're watching from heaven with that beautiful smile. Thank you for championing me, believing in me, and shaping so much of who I am. I miss you deeply, and I pray I always make you proud.

To my father, Jorge Piña—I thank God for the privilege of knowing you, and for the honor of leading you to Jesus in Peru. I know you are with him now, rejoicing.

To my sister, Evelyn Perez—I love you with all my heart. Thank you for always being there for me.

To my Aunt Nani and Uncle Ernest—you placed my first Bible in my hands, and that simple act redirected the course of my entire life. Thank you for your love and for planting the seeds of faith that brought me to this moment.

To my siblings on my father's side—you mean more to me than you will ever know. No matter where we are in the world, whenever we're together, joy follows. Thank you for loving me and for making every memory count.

To my Velez and Martinez families—you are treasures in my life. Thank you for believing in me and cheering me on. To God be the glory!

To my U-Turn Covenant Church family, staff, board of directors, pastoral team, soldiers of the cross, and my right-hand man, Edwin Gonzalez—you have walked with me through every battle, every breakthrough, and every tear. Thank you for standing in my corner, supporting my family, and pouring love into my life. You are part of this book.

To Peter Avilés—thank you for adopting me as your spiritual son. Your wisdom and encouragement breathed life into this vision long before it became a manuscript. The hours you spent talking with me about *Evangelship* will stay with me forever.

To Robert Guerrero and the Avance Cohort—you helped shape my thinking, stretch my perspective, and refine the heart of this book. Thank you for your guidance, your friendship, and for introducing me to Alan Hirsch. *Seguimos pa'lante, mi hermano en Cristo. A Dios sea la gloria!*

To Rico Altiery, Edwin Melendez, Josué Vázquez, Lou Mercado, Sean Sloan, Michael Carrion, Eli Gutierrez, Diter Aguilar, Alex Lugo, Efrain Muñoz, Bishop Ramfis Moulier, Tommy Torres, and to all my brothers from another mother—you know who you are. Thank you for years of encouragement, laughter, and ministry; you are more than friends—you are my brothers.

To Dr. Wilfredo "Choco" De Jesús, Dr. Jay Pike, and Dr. Price—your influence is woven into these pages. Thank you for the many hours of counsel, prayer, and encouragement before this was ever a book.

To the spiritual fathers who guided me early in my walk—Pastor Willie, Pastor Antonio Plá, and Dr. Raúl Marrero—thank you for pouring into me, discipling me, correcting me, and calling out God's purpose in me. Even now, as you stand face-to-face with Jesus, your impact endures. Thank you for loving me through every season, even my failures. *Los amo mucho, y los extraño también.*

To Liberty Christian Center and Pastora Millita—thank you for being my family from the beginning. I will never forget where I came from, and I thank you for loving me through every chapter of my journey.

To my in-laws, Angel and Gladys Quiñones—you are two of the most beautiful souls in my life. Thank you for believing in me, supporting Yezenia and me, and helping us pursue this dream.

To Sree and Laxmi Deshabathini—your encouragement, support, and faith in this project helped carry me through more than you know. *Evangelship* exists in part because you helped me keep going.

To Tori Thatcher, my first editor—thank you for helping me translate academic thought and life experience into words on a page. Your coaching and skills were invaluable.

To Anna and Rich Robinson and the entire 100Movements team—thank you for believing in this vision. Anna, your patience, insight, and editorial excellence helped shape this manuscript into a message I believe will impact this generation.

And finally, to Alan Hirsch—thank you for believing in me. You were the one who spoke life into this dream at a dinner table. Your encouragement and generosity paved the way for this book. Thank you for making room for my voice.

notes

introduction

1   A *barrio* is a Spanish-speaking quarter of a town or city.

2   Lawrence D. Perez, "Evangelship: Mobilizing a Culture of Discipleship that Leads to Evangelism in a Multiethnic Latino Context" (DMin diss., Southeastern University, 2024), https://firescholars.seu.edu/dmin/44.

1   inhale, exhale

1   Bob Deffinbaugh, "Israel's Relationship to the World," Bible.org, February 5, 2007, https://bible.org/seriespage/israels-relationship-world.

2   Simon Sinek, *Start with Why: How Great Leaders Inspire Everyone to Take Action* (New York: Portfolio, 2011).

3   Barna Group, *Reviving Evangelism: Current Realities That Demand a New Vision for Sharing Faith* (Ventura, CA: Barna Group, 2019), 10.

4   Dallas Willard, *Living in Christ's Presence: Final Words on Heaven and the Kingdom of God* (Downers Grove, IL: IVP, 2017),16.

5   Dr. Robert E. Coleman, *The Master Plan of Evangelism* (Grand Rapids, MI: Spire, 2010), 31.

6   Jeffrey Howell Lynn, "Making Disciples of Jesus Christ: Investigating, Identifying and Implementing an Effective Discipleship System" (DMin diss., Liberty University, 2014), 5.

7   Alan Hirsch, *Disciplism: Reimagining Evangelism Through the Lens of Discipleship* (Richmond, VA: 100Movements Publishing, 2024), 10.

2   ignite heart-level transformation

1   Frank Viola, *48 Laws of Spiritual Power: Uncommon Wisdom for Greater Ministry Impact* (Carol Stream, IL: Tyndale Momentum, 2022), eBook, 279.

2   Dallas Willard. *The Divine Conspiracy: Rediscovering Our Hidden Life in God* (San Francisco: HarperSanFrancisco, 1998), 34.

3   live questionably

1   Rodney Stark, *The Rise of Christianity: How the Obscure, Marginal Jesus Movement Became the Dominant Religious Force in the Western World in a Few Centuries* (Princeton, NJ: HarperOne, 1996), 161.

2   Michael Frost, *Surprise the World: The Five Habits of Highly Missional People* (Colorado Springs, CO: NavPress, 2016), 11–13.

3   Rodney Stark, *The Rise of Christianity: A Sociologist Reconsiders History* (Princeton, NJ: HarperOne, 1996), 81–89, 97–98, 118–22, 161.

4   Eugene H. Peterson, *Practice Resurrection: A Conversation on Growing Up in Christ* (Grand Rapids, MI: Eerdmans, 2010), 12.

5   Frost, *Surprise the World*, 14.

6   Frost, *Surprise the World*, 20–21.

4   don't discount yourself

1   Rick Richardson, *Behaviors of Your Evangelism Culture* (Orlando, FL: Exponential, 2022), 8.

2   Mark Russell, "*The Use of Business in Missions in Chiang Mai, Thailand*" (PhD diss., Asbury Theological Seminary, 2008).

3   Barna Group, *Reviving Evangelism*, 90.

4   Dave Ferguson and Jon Ferguson, *B.L.E.S.S.: 5 Everyday Ways to Love Your Neighbor and Change the World* (Washington, D.C.: Salem Books, 2021), 26.

5   Ed Stetzer, "Why Professional Evangelism Is Hurting the Church," *Outreach Magazine*, May 8, 2016, https://outreachmagazine.com/features/17219-why-professional-evangelism-is-hurting-the-church.html.

6   Erwin Raphael McManus, *Seven Frequencies of Communication: The Hidden Language of Human Connection* (Los Angeles, CA: The Arena Publishing, 2024), 23.

7   McManus, *Seven Frequencies of Communication*, 24.

5   be a story catcher

1   Eugene H. Peterson, *The Contemplative Pastor: Returning to the Art of Spiritual Direction* (Grand Rapids, MI: Eerdmans, 1989), 106.

2   David Augsburger, *Caring Enough to Hear and Be Heard: How to Hear and How to Be Heard in Equal Communication* (Ventura, CA: Regal Books, 1982), 19.

3   The shift from the third-person pronouns ("they") to the first-person ("we") beginning in Acts 16:10 is widely understood by scholars as evidence that Luke, the author of Acts, joined Paul's missionary team at Troas. See F. F. Bruce, *The Book of the Acts* (Grand Rapids, MI: Eerdmans, 1988), 307; and Darrell L. Bock, *Acts* (Grand Rapids, MI: Baker Academic, 2007), 531.

6   go where the people are

[1]   Paul G. Hiebert, "Conversion, Culture and Cognitive Categories," *Gospel in Context* 1, no. 4 (October 1978): 24–29; revised and expanded in Paul G. Hiebert, *Anthropological Reflections on Missiological Issues* (Grand Rapids, MI: Baker Academic, 1994), 107–36. See also Perez, "Evangelship: Mobilizing a Culture of Discipleship that Leads to Evangelism in a Multiethnic Latino Context," 44; Mark D. Baker, *Centered-Set Church: Discipleship and Community Without Judgmentalism* (Downers Grove, IL: IVP Academic, 2022), 21; W. Jay Moon, *Intercultural Discipleship: Learning from Global Approaches to Spiritual Formation*, illustrated edition (Grand Rapids, MI: Baker Academic, 2017), 46–47.

[2]   Jill L. Hurley, "Understanding Christian Conversion as a Post-Relational Ontological (RE) Turn to Relations," *OKH Journal: Anthropological Ethnography and Analysis Through the Eyes of Christian Faith* 2, no. 2 (July 30, 2018): 3, https://doi.org/10.18251/okh.v2I2.27.

7   find people of peace

[1]   Quoted in Myles Werntz, "The Immigration Stories We Don't See," *Christianity Today*, March 18, 2025. https://www.christianitytoday.com/2025/03/immigration-stories-we-do-not-see-migrant-god-review-villegas/.

8   build friendships of purpose

[1]   Hirsch, *Disciplism*, 9–10.

[2]   Ralph Moore, "Disciple Making That Reproduces," Discipleship.org, accessed October 29, 2025, https://discipleship.org/bobbys-blog/disciple-making-reproduction/.

[3]   Hirsh, *Disciplism*, 13.

[4]   Hirsch, *Disciplism*, 12.

[5]   Leonard Sweet, *Nudge: Awakening Each Other to the God Who's Already There* (Colorado Springs, CO: David C. Cook, 2010), 28.

9   walk together

[1]   Dietrich Bonhoeffer, *Life Together: The Classic Exploration of Christian Community*, translated by John W. Doberstein (San Francisco: HarperOne, 2009), 18–23.

[2]   Bonhoeffer, *Life Together*, 19.

3   For more information on the "one another" commands in the New Testament, see Jeffrey Kranz, "All the 'one another' commands in the NT [infographic]," March 9, 2014, https://overviewbible.com/one-another-infographic/.

10 persevere in hard seasons

1   Paul David Tripp, *Dangerous Calling: Confronting the Unique Challenges of Pastoral Ministry* (Wheaton, IL: Crossway, 2012), 23.

2   Henri J. M. Nouwen, *In the Name of Jesus: Reflections on Christian Leadership* (New York, NY: Crossroads, 1989), 62.

11 shoot every arrow

1   Lesslie Newbigin, *The Gospel in a Pluralist Society* (Grand Rapids, MI: Eerdmans, 1989), 233.

2   Dallas Willard, *The Great Omission* (New York, NY: HarperOne, 2006), 61.

3   I first heard this powerful nugget of insight from my friend David Hernandez during a NewLife Covenant Church Men's Retreat (October 2022).

12 be the event

1   Jerry Trousdale, *Miraculous Movements: How Hundreds of Thousands of Muslims Are Falling in Love with Jesus* (Nashville, TN: Thomas Nelson, 2012).

2   24:14 Multiplying Movements Together, "Global Movement Statistics," accessed November 24, 2025, https://2414now.net/wp-content/uploads/2025/06/2414-Dashboard.pdf.

about the author

Dr. Lawrence "Larry" Perez is the founder and senior pastor of U-Turn Covenant Church in Northlake, Illinois, with additional campuses in Chicago and Orlando.

Larry's first love is discipleship, evangelism, and developing emerging leaders—as a pastor, speaker, and teacher. He is an ordained minister with the Assemblies of God, a director of the Church Coaching Network for CORE Inc, and a ministry coach for the Chicago Partnership (TCP).

His ministry journey includes serving as national youth director for Young Defenders Ministry and as a trustee for MCIN, a global discipleship movement. Larry holds a BA in Communications (Northeastern Illinois University), an MA in Christian Ministry (Northern Seminary), and a DMin (Southeastern University).

The writing of *Evangelship* unfolded amidst a challenging personal season. While completing his doctoral work, he cared for his mother until her passing in 2023. In 2024, two weeks after submitting his dissertation, Larry survived a heart attack that led to a quadruple bypass surgery. He completed his degree, continued pastoring faithfully, and later that same year, laid his father to rest.

Through profound loss, miraculous survival, and unwavering perseverance, Larry emerged with a conviction that *Evangelship* is a timely, essential message needed to accelerate and advance the Great Commission in today's world.

Larry lives in Illinois with his wife, Yezenia, and their three children.

Learn more at www.evangelship.com.

Discover More Online:
Go deeper on evangelship with Larry Perez. Scan the QR code for free 10-minute small group video sessions, complete with discussion questions.
www.evangelship.com